SOLIDARITY IN A SLUM

·

SOLIDARITY

IN A SLUM

Joseph B. Tamney

A SCHENKMAN PUBLICATION

HALSTED PRESS DIVISION

JOHN WILEY & SONS

New York — London — Sydney — Toronto

Copyright © 1975
Schenkman Publishing Company, Inc.
Cambridge, Massachusetts 02138

Distributed solely by Halsted Press, a Division of
John Wiley & Sons, Inc., New York.

Library of Congress Cataloging in Publication Data

Tamney, Joseph B
    Solidarity in a slum.

    1. Milwaukee — Social conditions.   2. Solidarity — Case studies
  3 Slums — Milwaukee.   I. Title.
HN80.M58T35   301.18'028   74-5353
ISBN 0-470-84485-X
ISBN 0-470-84486-8 (pbk.)

Contents

Preface

The work reported here was made possible by a grant from the United Community Services of Milwaukee for the purpose of determining which residents of an area scheduled for urban renewal needed professional help from existing government agencies. The questionnaire used in the study reflected both the needs of United Fund and my professional interest in the problem of solidarity, or involvement; this monograph was influenced more by the latter than by the former.

The first chapter sets forth a theory of involvement. Although most of the propositions stated in this chapter are not tested by the research reported here, the theory provides the framework for the entire analysis that follows. The theory is referred to from time to time, and the choice of issues studied is better understood if the reader has first read it. This monograph represents not so much a test as an expansion of the theory.

Essentially, then, this work is an attempt to elaborate a theory of involvement.

I would like to thank the graduate students who worked so hard on this research project—Mr. John Musick, who was in charge of field operations; Mr. Ronald Manderscheid and Ms. Carol Coddeta, who helped on the analysis of data; and Messrs. John Rasmann and George Gerharz, whose theses I have made use of in this monograph. To these associates I owe a great deal.

Marquette University allowed free and frequent use of their computer facilities, for which I am grateful.

I would especially like to thank Mr. Peter Sheldon of United Fund for his cooperation.

1

The Study of Involvement

It is a fact that people live and die in virtual contact with only a small part of the world around them. A mother will cry about the troubles of her son who lives thousands of miles away, but remain unaffected by what happens to the poor, lonely, man living upstairs. Many will rejoice when their favorite football team wins the championship, but remain unmoved when someone discovers a cure for cancer. A fight between our son and a neighbor's child will arouse our emotions for hours; a war between distant African peoples does not affect us even for seconds. The people around us come and go, suffer and rejoice, live and die. But we are affected by little of all this; we are involved with few of the billions who surround us. The movie documentary delineates the approaching starvation of millions—we frown; the hero dies in the last reel of a melodrama—we cry. Each of us feels a sense of oneness, or, *involvement,* with only a few of the people and objects we encounter in life. This book is concerned with mapping the pattern of involvement—the pattern of threads binding humans together—that exists among the people living in one part of urban America.

WHAT IS INVOLVEMENT?

Involvement implies a sense of oneness. The type of experience referred to might be described with words other than "oneness." Individuals might describe themselves as "close;" they might feel "dependent;" a wife might say she is "chained" to her husband, or a husband might believe himself "dominated" by his job. The words in quotes connote different degrees of acceptance of a relationship, but they share the idea of oneness.

This same idea has been significant in the history of sociology. Durkheim described solidarity as follows: "it is impossible for men to live together, associating in industry, without acquiring a sentiment of the whole formed by their union, without attaching themselves to that whole, preoccupying themselves with its interests, and taking account of it in their conduct."[1] This "sentiment of the whole" is identical to a sense of oneness. Similarly, Cooley described the primary group as a "fusion of individualities in a common whole,"[2] Weber described solidarity as a subjective feeling of belonging together,[3] and Freud described identification as a process in which children become parents. All of these authors referred to an event characterized by a sense of oneness among two or more human beings.

It might be asked why we do not use the term solidarity or primary group rather than involvement. Just about all sociological theories on the primary group and solidarity have a positive bias that this study desires to avoid. Obviously, people can be deeply but negatively involved with each other, i.e., they can hate each other. But sociologists tend to avoid this possibility. When Faris discussed the primary group, one of whose characteristics is mutual sympathy, he opposed it to institutions, which are characterized by a sense of impersonal distance.[4] There is mention of "the hostile group", but what this means is not clear, although it seems to refer to an enemy with whom there need not be much involvement. Faris's vocabulary in the article referred to does not include a concept for intense negative involvement. Similarly, Weber used solidarity to refer to the absence of conflict;[5] and in a recent work by Cousins—"The concept of solidarity... [means] the relative preponderance of favorable over hostile affects, and a similar balance of moral respect (as over against moral condemnation), among the co-participants in the concrete group...."[6] In both the primary-group tradition and the solidarity tradition there is a positive bias; it is assumed that oneness is a happy condition. Hate and conflict are avoided. By using the term involvement it is hoped that this positive bias will be minimized. A condition of high involvement can be either positive or negative.[7]

WHAT INVOLVEMENT IS NOT

Involvement is not to be equated with any concept primarily referring to norms or satisfaction or success.

For instance, consider the term anomie. This is meant to describe a situation in which people have no norms, i.e., no socially agreed upon rules for the conduct of human affairs. It is necessary to understand that anomie is not the same as alienation. Consider the condition immediately after an earthquake. Two of the most important characteristics of such occasions are the absence of any consensus as to what is to be done (anomie) and the presence of a general sense of closeness among the victims (involvement).

It will be suggested later that high involvement is more likely when behavior is spontaneous. This would mean that, in general, the social situation likely to produce the most intense involvement will be anomic, i.e., one lacking in rules and regulations.

In other situations of course anomie and alienation go together. Sommer and Osmond have described "the schizophrenic no-society," i.e., the schizophrenic ward of a hospital, where there is no leadership or interdependence and which has no status system of its own or system of justice. "If further evidence is needed that the concept of a society cannot be appropriately applied to the way of life found on the long-stay wards of the mental hospital there is the fact that patients have very little interest in one another. Patients who have lived together on the same ward for many years do not even know each other's names; sociometric studies have shown that only a handful of reciprocated friendships occur; occupational therapists have compared patients doing craftwork to seven or eight people playing solitaire."[8] No structure, no rules, no interest—the patient ward can be described as both anomic and without involvement. In short, anomie, the absence of norms, and alienation, the absence of involvement, may or may not occur together; there is no necessary relation between them such that the presence of one condition requires either the presence or absence of the other. Anomie and alienation are quite distinct problems.

Similarly, a distinction must be made between satisfaction, or concepts based on satisfaction, such as morale, and involvement. It has already been pointed out that involvement may be either positive or negative. A son may be deeply conscious of his dissatisfaction with his mother, even to the point of murdering her. Obviously, the very fact that murder, which is the elimination of a relationship, would even be considered indicates that the son felt deeply involved with his mother. This mother-son relationship, then, would be characterized by low satisfaction and high involvement. Similarly, Bettelheim has described how some political prisoners in the German concentration camps emulated their gestapo guards.[9] These prisoners certainly were involved with their guards, but we can not imagine they were very satisfied with this relationship. High involvement, therefore, does not always mean high satisfaction.

Conversely, it is also possible to have high satisfaction and low involvement. A student might ask his teacher whether he is satisfied with his academic performance. The teacher need not be very involved with the student in order to answer "yes."

Usually, satisfaction simply indicates the extent to which a situation meets our expectations. Where our expectations are met or exceeded we are satisfied. Of course we may change our expectations so that we may find ourselves in the very same situation again, and feel quite dissatisfied. But the idea of expectation is not part of our concept of involvement, which is why satisfaction and involvement are quite distinct phenomena.[10]

Finally, concepts that are based on the idea of success are not to be equated with involvement. Consider the idea of integration, which refers to the efficiency of social arrangements in accomplishing their goals.[11] An interest in integration might lead to a study of consistency among the norms held by an aggregate of people, or of the extent to which people are motivated to conform to existing norms, or of the necessity of some deviance from shared norms in order to achieve the aggregate's goals. This work is concerned with none of these problems. Efficiency and involvement are distinct problems. For instance it has been argued that governmental stability requires some apathy; it is assumed that if everyone were interested in all the problems faced by government so much time would be spent in discussing these problems with concerned citizens and so many different solutions would be put forth that government would be unable to take decisive actions quickly enough. It remains an open question whether this is true or not. However, the argument clearly assumes that success and involvement are distinct, since it suggests that continuously high citizen involvement might be inefficient. Likewise, we hear of doctors' refusing to operate on their loved ones; the assumption is that they are too involved to be able to do the job with the greatest efficiency. Success is quite distinct from a sense of oneness.

Involvement, then, is not to be equated with any concept that refers to norms, satisfaction, or success.

It is possible to ask four distinct questions of an aggregate of people: How involved are they with each other? How anomic is the aggregate? How satisfied are the people with their way of life? How efficient are they in achieving their goals? This work is concerned with only the first question.

As previously noted this work is concerned with mapping the pattern of involvement among an aggregate of people. Before doing this, however, some basic theoretical ideas about involvement will be presented. This will serve as a background for the analysis that follows in later chapters.

SOURCES OF INVOLVEMENT

Perhaps there is no stronger source of involvement than the experience of physical union with another, as in giving birth to a child or in sexual intercourse. We consider a baby to be physically part of the mother. Even after the two are separated, a recognition of having been part of the mother makes the child feel involved with her. It is important to recognize the total irrelevance of the time dimension in the theory of involvement. Spatial identity is a source of involvement, whether that identity took place in the past, is occurring this moment, or is anticipated as a future event.

It is not difficult to understand why spatial identity can produce a sense of oneness. There are laws of perception that organize or unify the field of experience. "Elements in experience are automatically and almost irresistibly grouped—other things equal—according to proximity, similarity and continuity."[12] When two objects like foetus and mother are so close and continuous we see them as one. The manner in which human beings perceive their environment makes physical closeness a source of involvement.

Our first theorem, therefore, is: *The extent of involvement depends on the physical distance between objects.* Physical union represents one extreme on the continuum of physical distance. In general as distance declines the sense of involvement should increase. However, at present the exact relation between involvement and distance is unknown. This is true in two senses: 1) We do not know how to translate units of distance into units of involvement, e.g., if A lives five yards away from C, and B lives ten yards away from C, does this mean that C is likely to feel twice as involved with A as with B? 2) We do not know the significance of the length of time a certain distance is maintained; previously it was stated that the time dimension is irrelevant, and this seems true in the sense that whether an event is associated with the past, present, or future seems irrelevant; on the other hand the duration of the event might well be important; would a person not feel more involved with someone who lived nearby for five years than with someone who lived nearby for five days? The answer would seem to be "yes," but it is now impossible to predict the size of the difference in involvement resulting from these two cases.

That we commonly express involvement in terms of distance seems meaningful. People often say about their friends—"we are very close." Conversely, we describe people who are indifferent to us as "detached" or "distant." Using the distance analogy is probably the most common means of expressing degrees of involvement. This fact certainly supports the idea that physical closeness is a source of involvement. If it were not what would explain the appeal of the analogy?

It is relevant that among other species there exist mechanisms for maintaining a relationship between distance and involvement. It would seem hazardous to suggest that *homo sapiens* has lost all sense of a relationship between distance and involvement. Carpenter has written that: "An important clue to social relations in primate societies is the observed spatial relations of individuals, sub-groups, and organized groups. The strength of the attachments between two individuals may be judged, or actually measured, by observing for a period of time the average distance which separates the two animals."[13] In general vertebrates maintain congruence between proximity and involvement.[14] Given the continued usage of the distance analogy it seems quite likely that this association between proximity and involvement is continued by *homo sapiens.*

But the discussion has really pointed our that proximity is related to involvement in two ways: as source and as symbol. To the extent that two people live close to each other or approach the foetus-mother situation, they are likely to feel a sense of oneness. But it also seems true that the closer two people live to each other the more they believe they should feel involved, since distance is supposed to symbolize oneness. To live close to someone and not be involved with them is likely to generate a sense of living a lie. But if closeness is a source of involvement how is it possible not to feel involved with, say, our neighbors? In other words, if closeness is not only a symbol, but a source, of involvement, how is it possible to "live a lie"? It is possible if closeness is more potent as a symbol of involvement than as a source of involvement. And we suspect that this is the case. The everyday use of the distance analogy suggests that closeness is a powerful symbol of involvement, while the already legendary apathy of urban neighbors indicates that closeness is at best a weak source of involvement.

It could be that the symbolic significance of distance has been lost in the urban environment. The distance analogy might be truly meaningless to urbanites—a linguistic anachronism. This is a matter for empirical study.

There are, then, two theorems relating distance and involvement: *The extent of involvement depends on the physical distance between objects. The extent to which people believe objects should be involved depends on the physical distance between objects.*

Durkheim wrote about two sources of solidarity—similarity and interdependence. Freud discussed two bases of love: 1) narcissistic—when the other person resembles us as we are or were or would be; and 2) functional—when the other person gives us what we need, such as tenderness or protection. Freud made the important point that for similarity to be a source of involvement the time dimension is not important, i.e., the similarity need not relate to us as we are now to produce involvement. On the whole, however, Freud's scheme is similar to Durkheim's formulation. Toennies in discussing human relations distinguished: 1) friendship—"the simplest fellowship type is represented by a pair who live together in a brotherly, comradely, and friendly manner, and it is most likely to exist when those involved are of the *same* age, sex and sentiment or engaged in the *same* activity or have the *same* intentions, or when they are united by *one* idea" (italics mine); and 2) the authoritative type, such as the relation between a father and son. Toennies talks more about dominance than interdependence, but all three theorists stressed that involvement is related to similarity and power (this is a broad term meant to include both interdependence and domination).[14]

Less well known, but more original, is Simmel's work on the anaysis of relationship. He emphasized that relationships are based on knowing something about another, and that differences in intensity of relationships are due

SOLIDARITY IN A SLUM

to differences in the degree people reveal themselves to one another.[16] Unfortunately, Simmel did not discuss the implications of his approach for the previously developed theories of Durkheim and Toennies.

It is true that Toennies frequently referred to understanding, but as his translator notes: *"Verstandnis* is translated 'understanding.' The concept ... should also carry the meaning of mutual understanding and possession of similar sentiments, hopes, aspirations, desires, attitudes, emotions, and beliefs."[17] For Toennies understanding was a consequence of similarity. The value of Simmel's work is that it stresses the independent importance of knowledge as a basis of relationship. It is true that when there is consciously recognized similarity, there is understanding. But the presence of understanding does not require similarity; people can know something about each other without being similar.

It is possible to pull together from the sociological classics, then, a third theorem: *The extent of involvement depends on the amount of similarity, power, and knowledge.*[18]

The idea of three social sources of involvement is tenable, for each is a way of being another. If two people are similar, they are, to a degree, the same. Likewise, if one person has power over another, the subordinate becomes the concrete embodiment of the purpose existing in the mind of the power-wielder; in a way, therefore, the slave is the master and vice-versa. Finally, to the extent we know someone that person exists in our minds, and we are the other. Similarity, power, and knowledge represent three ways of being another.

The willingness to communicate seems related to these same three variables. People tend not to start relationships; most communication is confirmation or elaboration of a pre-existing relation. When two sports-car owners drive past each other, they often feel free to honk their horns and wave, especially when their type of car first appears on the market; the similarity of ownership makes this sign of recognition acceptable. When a new employee reports at the job, he does not hesitate to talk to the boss; the work organization already relates them via power. It is not unusual to hear a conversation begin: "You don't know me, but I have heard a lot about you...." In this case knowledge legitimates communication. Goffman has suggested that "as a general rule... acquainted persons [i.e., people who know each other] in a social situation require a reason not to enter a face engagement with each other, while unacquainted persons require a reason to do so."[19] When people are already related because of similarity, power or knowledge then communication is legitimate and, according to Goffman, recognition of the relation is required. Under such conditions, to communicate is simply to activate a latent bond. The relative ease of communication when one of these three social sources is present supports the theorem that these are sources of involvement.

An attempt was made to test this third theorem in a study of reactions to the death of President Kennedy.[20] It was assumed that the extent to which people were affected by this event was a measure of their involvement in Kennedy. Some relationships were found between this measure and indicators of ideal similarity, power, and knowledge in the Kennedy-respondent relations. The study distinguished between real similarity and ideal similarity; this was based on Freud's distinction between people being like us as we act, or being like what we would like to be, i.e., being similar to our ideals. This is a valuable distinction not made use of by many sociologists. Although this research did produce some significant statistical associations the overall results were far from giving complete support to the theorem. For instance, the social sources of involvement worked differently for males and females, i.e., not all three sources were significantly related to the assassination-reaction measure for both males and females; power was significant for males but not females. This study does suggest, however, that the third theorem might be a useful source of empirical work.

IMAGINARY AND SENSED ENVIRONMENTS

All human beings live in at least two worlds—the internal or imaginary and the external or perceived. For all practical purposes it can be said that human beings exist in two environments simultaneously—the imagination and the perceived world.

But for many people the fact of a simultaneous existence in two environments is not a real problem. The people they think about are the people they live with. A mother might be sitting at home and at one moment talking with her daughter and in the next daydreaming about her daughter. But, on the other hand, a mother might at one moment be talking with her husband and in the next reminiscing about her last meeting with her lover. That some sense of alienation is natural and universal because man is an imaginative creature is important to know but not of primary interest to sociologists. On the other hand the extent to which objects occur in both the imaginary and perceived worlds varies considerably from person to person and culture to culture, and therefore is of interest to sociologists. Among the members of a farm family there is probably a high degree of overlap between the people perceived and the people imagined. But what happens, for instance, when a farm boy moves away to the "big city"? At least for awhile he will tend to live in two different worlds—the perceived city and the imagined farm. Or compare modern adolescents and adults. The former are more likely to be dreamers—imagining a trip to the moon, a date with a movie star, becoming famous, and so on. The adolescent lives in more "worlds" than the adult. What is the effect of this on involvement? It is probable that when people live in more than one world, or environment, they can never feel as involved in any one of these environments,

SOLIDARITY IN A SLUM

as can someone who has experienced only one locality and one set of human beings. We suggest, therefore, the general idea that: *The extent of involvement depends on the degree of overlap between the imaginary and sensed environments.* In other words alienation can be reduced either by fantasizing only about the perceived environment or by perceiving only objects from the fantasized environment (e.g., the person who becomes Napoleon).

THEORY OF DISENGAGEMENT

There is one theory of involvement that is relevant here, but which does not seem reducible to the theorems presented in this chapter—the theory of disengagement.

It has been suggested that as people become old they disengage themselves from society. What does this mean? What is the relation between disengagement and involvement?

Disengagement sounds like the absence of involvement, and this theory would seem to suggest that as people grow old they become alienated. But this is not an accurate rendition of the above theory. Cumming elaborated on the meaning of engagement as follows: "The fully-engaged person acts in a large number and wide variety of roles in a system of divided labor, and feels an obligation to meet the expectations of his role partners. ...Roughly, the depth and breadth of a man's engagement can be measured by the degree of potential disruption that would follow his sudden death."[21] There are several dimensions to the meaning of engagement: 1) the number of roles, 2) the variety of roles, 3) the degree of felt obligation to meet the expectations of others, and 4) the power and uniqueness of the individual. Moreover, Cumming makes explicit that engagement is not merely activity—"activity and engagement are not in the same dimension. A disengaged person often maintains a high level of activity in a small number and narrow variety of roles, although it is doubtful if it is possible to be at once firmly engaged and inactive."[22] There are several problems with Cumming's exploration because of the presence of unjustified assumptions. She assumes that a person's significance for a group is a measure of variety of roles, but surely this is unwarranted; a government official may "bury himself in his work" and thus be both significant and restricted regarding role variety. Moreover Cumming's assumption that engaged people are more conforming would seem to reflect more the conservative bias in favor of conformity than known facts. If we eliminate these assumptions, then, engagement can be reduced to the number and variety of roles a person plays.

Translated into presently relevant terms the theory suggests that old people become involved in fewer objects.[23] (The idea of "variety" is dropped because its meaning is not clear.)

But as Cumming elaborates her ideas she goes beyond the rather narrow description of aging as becoming involved in fewer objects. She, also, describes the change from middle to old age as a move from organic to mechanical solidarity. "Immediately after retirement, husbands seem redundant to many women who have developed lives of their own since the termination of child-raising. However, extremely old people, with no division of labor at all, become dependent upon one another to such an extent that if one dies the other is likely to follow quickly. This special case of a very binding mechanical solidarity is probably the result of these extremely old people being almost merged into one identity like twin infants."[24] Aging means a shift in the dominant basis of involvement from power to similarity.

According to Cumming, then, aging means that people are involved with fewer objects and that the dominant basis of the relationships that do exist is similarity.

Why does aging have these effects? Obviously working people are forced to retire, and this might lower the number of objects people are involved with, but this could be only a temporary condition. Retirement itself does not necessitate a prolonged decline in the number of objects in which a person is involved. But Cumming does suggest that in the American industrial society retirement is a prolonged problem because: a) many working people in such a society find no leisure-time activities that use the same skills developed by their work; there is no continuity, therefore, between work and the post-retirement leisure activities available; and b) in the American industrial society retirement tends to mean failure.[25] But why should (a) lead to prolonged disengagement? The first argument would seem to be significant only if other conditions were causing a decline in general interest in the environment; (b) might be such a condition, but let us postpone comment on this argument for a moment.

Cumming also suggested that disengagement might begin "sometime during middle life when certain changes of perception occur, of which the most important is probably an urgent new perception of the inevitability of death. ... It is quite possible that a vivid apprehension of mortality—perhaps when the end of life seems closer than its start—is the beginning of the process of growing old."[26] It seems to me that the argument suggested here is that in the face of death people begin to withdraw; but, why is this limited to disengagement, that is, why does not the fact of death produce general alienation rather than simply a decline in the number of objects involved with? The same comment can be applied to the argument already presented, that retirement causes disengagement because it connotes failure. Why do not failure and the fact of death produce alienation and not simply disengagement?

Cumming's work, as she acknowledges, is not complete. It does, however, raise interesting questions and points to relevant variables. For instance, it suggests that failure and the realization of death might lead to withdrawal. On the other hand, why these should lead to only disengagement and not complete alienation is not clear. Finally, Cumming's work emphasizes the probability that as people age withdrawal in some form does occur.

This last point on aging and withdrawal is both confirmed and amended by the work of Rosenmayr and Kocheis. They write:

> The great practical and emotional significance of family relations—but at the same time old people's desire to keep at a distance—became obvious to us as early as 1957, from the initial phase of our gerontological studies in Vienna. This at first appeared paradoxical, but it soon became clear that precisely this wish *to maintain some distance but not to be isolated* was to be regarded as a typical attitude among the aged. The preference for a certain amount of segregation holds not only in the area of family relations; it can also be observed in the attitude of old people towards their local social environment. We have shown in detail that aged persons appreciate arrangements (e.g., of gardens and green spaces) where they are somewhat protected and withdrawn from their surroundings, but at the same time are able to take part in, or at least watch, what is going on. They want social contacts, but resent interference. It is a general attitude, which we characterized by the formula: 'Intimacy—but at a distance. ...'[27]

Rosenmayr and Kocheis's idea of 'intimacy at a distance' reminds us of Cumming's saying 'disengagement but not alienation.' These phrases are suggestive but lack precision. They both suggest that old age has a unique form of involvement that is somewhat short of complete involvement. Perhaps the application of the theory of involvement presented in this work might help to gain precision. The work of both Cumming and of Rosenmayr and Kocheis suggests that old people seek involvement on a basis other than physical closeness and power; so Rosenmayr and Kocheis, for instance, use the phrase "at a distance" and suggest that old people "resent interference." Cumming suggests that the desired basis is similarity, yet could it not be understanding? But the crucial question, still unanswered, is whether old people are more alienated in our sense than others.

There is another idea mentioned by Cumming which is worth noting. She writes: "a person with a store of memories is less likely to give full attention to the world around him than the person who has fewer symbolic residues to capture his attention."[28] This is interesting. Perhaps it is not that old people withdraw, but that they become less involved with objects in their perceivable environment and more involved with fantasy objects, like a dead spouse, a distant child, or an invisible God.

Studies of involvement in specific institutions tend not to support the idea of disengagement. Glenn and Grimes reported that, after holding constant the sex and education of people, just about as many aged people vote as people in their fifties. They conclude "our data provide no strong evidence that [voter] turnout typically increases after age 32."[29] Moreover, reported political interest seems to increase with age. However, the authors also note that the surveys they relied on might have missed the more senile, feeble old people; thus, their conclusions may be more positive than reality justified.

Moberg reviewed numerous studies on age and religious activity. He concluded: "Research to date seems to indicate fairly conclusively that ritualistic behavior outside the home tends to diminish with increasing age, while religious attitudes and feelings apparently increase among people who have an acknowledged religion." "In other words, religion as a set of external extradomiciliary rituals apparently decreases in old age, while the internal personal responses linked with man's relationships to God apparently increase among religious people. Thus both disengagement from and re-engagement with religion are typical in old age!"[30]

That aging people in some sense withdraw seems a worthwhile hypothesis. But what is the nature of this withdrawal—does it mean disengagement or complete alienation? Does it mean merely a change to a new basis of involvement? Does it mean a shift of involvement from the perceivable to the fantasy world? And, finally, if in some sense people do withdraw, why do they?

In review it seems that there has been presented a fairly well-developed general theory of involvement, but little understanding of how and why involvement is distributed the way it is in existing societies. The purpose of this work is to increase understanding of the distribution of involvement. Regarding the general theory of the sources of involvement, for the most part, its value will be simply assumed. Some remarks concerning this theory will be made, but the focus is on the distribution of involvement.

It should be emphasized that this work is not a study of norms about involvement. That certainly is an interesting project, but not the present purpose—which is to discover not with whom a person believes he should be involved, but with whom he actually is involved. Throughout a framework will be developed for the eventual emergence of a theory for the distribution of involvement.

The focus of this research, therefore, is on the pattern of involvement in an urban slum.

2

The People Studied

In the spring of 1966 we carried out a survey of residents in an area of Milwaukee scheduled for urban renewal. Data were collected from 748 respondents, but analysis concentrated on the 623 female homemakers who were interviewed. Question topics included in the survey related to such things as the fantasy life of the respondents as well as to their home life, their participation in voluntary associations and their involvement with the national government. These data will be analyzed in subsequent chapters,

The purpose of this chapter is to introduce the people of Kilbourntown, the urban renewal area in which the study took place. First, the physical neighborhood itself will be described. Second, some of the characteristics of the people interviewed will be discussed. The social characteristics presented in this chapter will be related in subsequent chapters to various aspects of our respondents' patterns of involvement. Third, there will be some concluding remarks on the relevance of the information presented in this chapter for a theory of involvement.

THE PLACE

Milwaukee fans out to the north, west, and south from a downtown area that begins on the shore of Lake Michigan. The inner core—the Negro area of the city—begins at the downtown area and extends somewhat west but mostly north. Figure 2-1 divides the inner core into three sections; the lowest third has the poorest families and the oldest homes; as one goes north everything gets better. Almost in the center of the poorest third of the inner core is the urban renewal area in which resided the subjects of this study. The project's

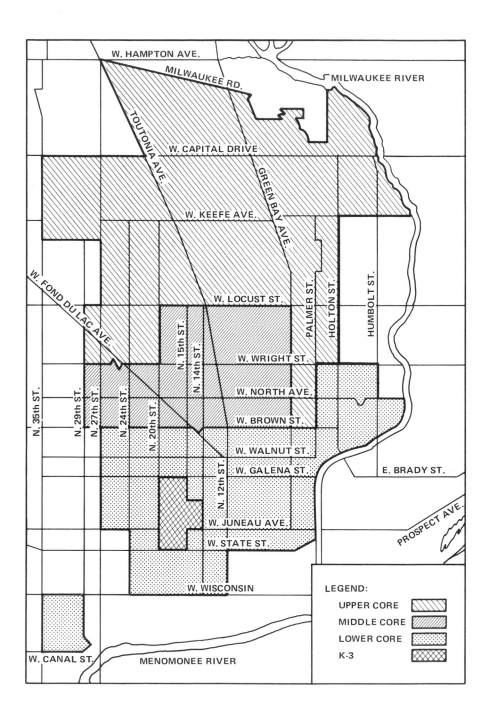

W. HAMPTON AVE.

MILWAUKEE RD.

MILWAUKEE RIVER

TOUTONIA AVE.

W. CAPITAL DRIVE

GREEN BAY AVE.

W. KEEFE AVE.

W. FOND DU LAC AVE.

PALMER ST.

HOLTON ST.

HUMBOLT ST.

W. LOCUST ST.

N. 15th ST.

N. 14th ST.

W. WRIGHT ST.

N. 35th ST.

N. 29th ST.

N. 27th ST.

N. 24th ST.

N. 20th ST.

W. NORTH AVE.

W. BROWN ST.

N. 12th ST.

W. WALNUT ST.

W. GALENA ST.

E. BRADY ST.

W. JUNEAU AVE.

PROSPECT AVE.

W. STATE ST.

W. WISCONSIN

LEGEND:

UPPER CORE

MIDDLE CORE

LOWER CORE

K-3

W. CANAL ST.

MENOMONEE RIVER

14

boundaries have little intrinsic meaning; they resulted from the location of previously inaugurated projects, the location of streets scheduled for expansion, and the requirement that a renewal area contain a government-specified minimum number of deficient homes. In its artificiality the area is representative of most politically defined units in a metropolitan region. This work is based, in part, on a study financed by the city renewal agency, which commissioned an investigation of the problems that existed among the people living in Kilbourntown (or K-3 for short).

The unifying architectural theme is sidewalk-porch. The proximity of pedestrian and porch puts strollers within easy eyesight and, in summertime, easy earshot of the inhabitants. Extending back and sometimes up from these porches are homes of varying sizes, shapes, and colors. They tend to be two-stories high[1] and range from drab, decrepit masses of peeling dirty white to structures of bright, freshly-painted trim and newly re-sided walls. The condemnation of every building in Kilbourntown ignored the wide range in quality of the residences. Some homes were decaying, while others indicated mighty salvage efforts. All have been destroyed. Because of the many attempts over the years to maintain or revive the buildings there is an amazing variety of textures—stone, wood, and various kinds of modern replacements for these standard materials. Variety of quality, variety of color, variety of material— variety is perhaps the key characteristic of the K-3 physical environment.

Scattered throughout the area are businesses of many kinds, especially grocery stores, and bars. But the main business street is Vliet Street. It is not a "stroll street." For instance, on one side of the street there is: a hat store, a restaurant, a store that sells restaurant machinery, a shoe store, a bar, a plumbing-supply store, a coffee shop, and a government office. Looking across the street you would see: a restaurant, a pet shop, a barbershop, a T.V.-repair store, a dry cleaners, a fuel-company office, a private house, and a hardware store. Vliet street contains very few stores likely to attract window-shoppers; in general, there are few reasons to stroll there. However, along the six blocks that are within the boundaries of K-3 there are fifteen bars and three churches. In all, Kilbourntown contains twenty-five bars and five churches. But often adjacent to these "community centers" are businesses completely unrelated to the neighborhood—such as the plumbing-equipment outlet, a wholesale meat store and the fuel company office. The area contains two extremes—the centers of liquor and religion and the non-neighborhood businesses—with little of the in-between types of establishments.

Figure 2-2 displays the street pattern and the traffic count on those streets for which the information was available. As the counts suggest, Milwaukee seems to pass in review for the residents. It is important to keep in mind, however, that few of these cars stop in the area; they simply pass through. The heavy use of streets does not knit the neighborhood into the city, but rather

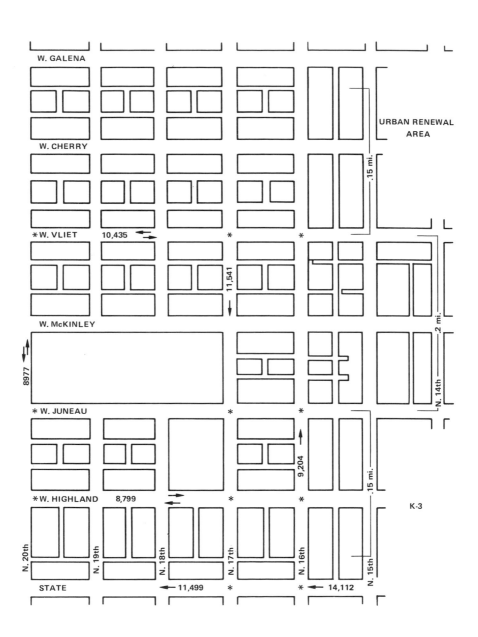

Figure 2-2. Numbers on map represent traffic counts for 24-hour periods in 1965 and 1966. Arrow indicates direction of traffic, stars indicate traffic lights. The area ends just south of Galena and north of State Streets. The dimensions of the area are indicated.

SOLIDARITY IN A SLUM

it tears Kilbourntown apart. The traffic segregates the blocks; it does not unify the city. Like many of the non-neighborhood stores the traffic pattern attracts strangers totally uninterested in the residents of the area.

Most of the low-lying buildings are dominated by over four hundred trees, which give a restful cast to the neighborhood. Unfortunately, there is an absence of pleasant spacing; it is boom or bust; some streets have no trees, others have them clustered so tightly that it is difficult for the sun to break through in summer.[2] This uneven distribution dissolves the area into patches of green and stretches of glare.

SAFETY

Of special importance if human beings are to maintain neighborhood relationships is a sense of security; residents must not fear venturing outside their homes. Most of Kilbourntown is situated in the Milwaukee police district that in 1965 had the highest number of murders, forcible rapes, assaults, and sex offences; there was no criminal category involving aggressive behavior in which this district did not have the highest incidence.

Among those persons convicted of aggressive, criminal behavior in 1965, fourteen individuals came from the households studied; thus in a single year just under 2 percent of the families to be discussed had one of their members convicted of aggressive, criminal behavior.[3]

Reprinted below is a story that appeared in the October 11, 1966, issue of the *Milwaukee Journal;* the Wells Street School is immediately adjacent to our area.

> Fear walks the streets near the Wells Street Junior High School at N. 19th and W. Wells Sts., particularly at night. It takes several forms:
> A 33 year old mother of three who says she is frightened goes from house to house seeking signatures on a petition for more police protection.
> Signers of the petition beg that their names not be disclosed lest there be retaliation from gangs of toughs who, they say, roam the area.
> The school is closed during the lunch hour. Pupils must remain inside, eating either a cold lunch brought from home or a hot one in the cafeteria.
> Every day, two or three pupils complain to school authorities that they have been punched or kicked by young hoodlums who hang around the Norris playground, just north of the school.
> A school monitor's eye is blackened by the toughs who, two or three times a week, enter the school.
> Broken glass is strewn to make "tires go, pop, pop." There is ugly profanity and open drinking on the streets.
> The petition circulator, a Negro, is waging a campaign for a tightly enforced curfew, more beat patrolmen, better street lighting and harsher punishment for the youthful offenders, who are also Negro.

"We are kind of petrified, more than scared," she said Monday. "It is like sitting on a keg of dynamite and not knowing when it is going to explode, but knowing it will if something isn't done."[4]

The present study offers no direct evidence concerning this matter; it might well be that the reporter exaggerated or even severely distorted the situation. Yet both the evidence on crime and this story do point to the absence of a degree of safety that is expected in our society and that is an important prerequisite for the development of involvement beyond a person's own household. Without safety, doors cease to be openings, and become barriers.

THE STUDY

An initial canvass made with the help of the local mailman showed that the renewal area contained 1,191 households (374 White, 730 Negro, 61 Spanish-speaking, 12 American Indian, and 4 Oriental). Because of a limited budget it was necessary to reduce the universe to 1,069 households; the dwellings north of Cherry Street (see Figure 2-2) were eliminated; this meant the loss almost exclusively of Negro families. For the 1,069 households we attempted to study, the results were as follows: completed: 748; vacant at the time of interview: 162; refused: 76; unable to contact (after 4 calls): 83. In short, one member from 82 percent of the households still occupied at the time of the study was interviewed.

To ensure as much cooperation and openness as possible we assigned an interviewer of the same ethnic background as the person to be inverviewed. The initial canvass revealed the proportion of each major ethnic group in K-3. We then gathered a staff of about twenty, which reflected these proportions; the interviewers were from the same general type of area as the respondents. They were hired through local agencies such as The Urban League, and trained by us.

Since the study was commissioned to gather information about entire households, the interviewers were instructed to always try to interview the housewife; it was assumed that she would be the single person who would know the most about an entire household.

Of the 748 people interviewed, 101 were males and 642 were females. The analysis reported here is based only on the women interviewed. Moreover, to achieve some basic similarity among the people analyzed, it was decided to eliminate the 19 cases in which the woman interviewed was not the homemaker. Usually "homemaker" meant simply the wife of the breadwinner (the respondent was asked to name the "breadwinner"). When this was inappropriate, either because there was no male breadwinner or because there was one but no wife was living with him, it was assumed that the adult woman in the household was the homemaker. If there was more than one adult women, the middle-aged woman was considered the homemaker; for instance, in a home that included a twenty, a forty, and a sixty year old woman, the forty year old was considered the homemaker. This study, then is about the households of 623 female homemakers in Kilbourntown. In the total sample of 748 households that we contacted, there was a total of 674 female homemakers. Our sample of 623 represents, therefore, 92 percent of the female homemakers in the homes contacted.[5] Remembering that we succeeded in interviewing only 82 percent of the households in K-3, this means that this study is based on a sample of 75-80 percent of the female homemakers in Kilbourntown; it is impossible to state the exact percentage because we do not know how many female homemakers there were in the households not contacted.

DESCRIPTION OF THE SAMPLE

RACE AND AGE. When we look at a large aggregate of people, there are three ways in which we can easily group them: by sex, age, or color. People are sorted out along these dimensions automatically, i.e., without thinking, because of the comparative visual obviousness of the categories for each of these three dimensions.

The multi-modal and bi-modal distributions of color and sex respectively make them "natural" dimensions for perceptual categorization.[6] Although age is more normally distributed, the obvious differences among young people, old people, and the rest of a population, as well as the frequency of the "extreme" cases, allow one to readily use these gross age-categories in grouping a population. Upon seeing an aggregate we would tend to divide them in terms of color, sex and age; it is not surprising, therefore, that social roles are frequently allocated on these same bases. Perceptual groupings on the basis of these three types of categories are "givens" upon which a society builds. One of the purposes of this study is to examine the extent to which these "perceptually given" groupings are sociologically meaningful.

Since all males were eliminated from this analysis, the interest is concentrated on color and age. Specifically, the study compares "whites" with "blacks", old people with those between the ages of twenty and sixty years. Since the sample includes only homemakers, the third age-category, children, is not relevant. Each chapter, then, begins with a comparison of whites and blacks, young and old.

Table 2–1 describes the female homemakers by color and age. As can be seen, the sample tends to be composed of old "whites" and young "blacks". There are relatively few Spanish-speaking and Indians, so our analysis will focus on the "whites" and "blacks." In comparing the latter two aggregates the differences in age distribution will have to be kept continually in mind.

Figure 2–3 shows the ratio of "whites" and "blacks" on each block in K-3.

THE PEOPLE STUDIED   19

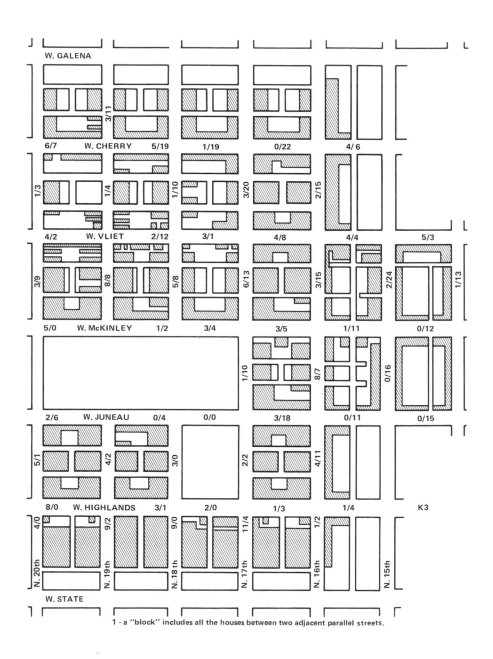

1 - a "block" includes all the houses between two adjacent parallel streets.

TABLE 2–1

AGE AND COLOR OF FEMALE HOMEMAKER RESPONDENTS (N=623)

(Figures given as percentages of total sample)

| Age | Color[1] | | | | |
	"White" (N=169)	"Black" (N=409)	Spanish-speaking (N=24)	Indian (N=9)	Other[2] (N=12)
17–19	2	3	4	0	0
20–29	7	33	21	33	25
30–39	15	27	50	33	33
40–49	15	17	13	22	25
50–59	20	8	8	11	8
60–74	28	9	4	—	8
75 plus	12	1	—	—	—
no response	2	2	—	—	—

1. We use "color" rather than "ethnicity," because the major part of our analysis is concerned with "skin-color aggregates." Our label, of course, is less appropriate for the Spanish-speaking or the Indians than for the rest of the sample. The respondent was categorized by the interviewer, who was given the following alternatives: White, Negro, Latin-American (Mexican, Puerto-Rican), Other (Indian, Chinese, etc.), and Indeterminate. Since we tried to ethnically match interviewer and interviewee the labelling was probably as accurate as is possible. "Black," for instance, means respondents were perceived as negroes by the interviewers.

2. Includes cases in which interviewer failed to designate ethnicity of respondent.

TABLE 2–2

LENGTH OF RESIDENCE AT PRESENT ADDRESS

Years	Percent (N=623)
1	34
2	13
3	11
4	7
5	4
6–10	11
11–20	11
21–57	6
No response	3

Neither the Spanish-speaking nor the Indians cluster on any one block. As can be seen on the map, "whites" tend to live in the western and especially southwestern part of Kilbourntown (i.e., toward the corner of 20th Street and State Street). Yet, "whites" are scattered throughout the renewal area. About 44 percent of them live on blocks that do not contain a majority of "whites." However, only 28 percent of the "whites" under forty years of age live on such blocks. The more integrated blocks tend to contain old "whites" and young "blacks." The presence of both color and age differences probably minimizes the development of involvement across racial lines, even though there is the bond of spatial proximity among those living on integrated streets.

The dominant impression of the K-3 residents is variety. There are "whites," blacks," Indians, Spanish-speaking, and a few Orientals. All the ages are represented. Both the buildings and the people of Kilbourntown lack any unifying theme.

MOBILITY.   One of the major characteristics of modern society is the extent to which people move about. But physical mobility is not a single variable. It breaks down into time-per-place and variety of places. An individual might move a great deal and thus spend little time with any one set of neighbors, but make all these moves within the same city, so that the general social and cultural atmosphere remains stable. The effects of such a pattern would seem to be quite different than if a person were a world traveller. The analysis, therefore, tries to separate the effects of time-per-place and of the social variety of places lived.

Tables 2-2 through 2-6 present the basic data on mobility. What stands out is the high mobility of the sample.[7]

Table 2-6 presents all four of the dimensions of mobility just discussed. As one reads down and to the right in the table, mobility as a significant experience declines. As can be seen in the upper left-hand corner of the table only 2 percent of the respondents are extremely mobile, that is, have lived at their present address less than five years, have moved four or more times in the last five years, have lived in Milwaukee less than ten years, and have lived in four or more different towns and cities. At the other extreme the figure is 14 percent. It is worth noting that 24 percent of the sample is very "cosmopolitan," i.e., has lived in four or more different towns and cities. Although Kilbourntown might be considered a slum, the residents are not to be thought of as individuals who have never left their block and know nothing of anything outside their own small world. Many of the K-3 residents have experienced quite different ways of life. Overall, there is no pattern in Table 2-6. The table simply documents the variety of mobility-experiences the respondents have had.

There has been some research on the relation between physical mobility and involvement. Litwak, based on a study of attitudes about involvement and not of involvement itself, concluded that mobility does not destroy extended family ties. Bott, on the other hand, emphasized that mobility pushes the nuclear family together; husband and wife depend on each other more, and have the same set of friends; they do things together. "In facing the external world, they draw on each other, for their strongest emotional investment is made where there is continuity." This idea that involvement is related to continuity is interesting. Bott's work suggests that although extended family ties exist among mobile people, they will not be very significant. In fact, although there is general agreement that such ties do exist, we do not know how much involvement these ties symbolize. Bott's idea that "emotional investment is made where there is continuity" seems worth further investigation. We shall return to this point.[3]

TABLE 2-3

YEARS LIVED IN MILWAUKEE

Years	Percent (N=623)
1	8
2–3	6
4–5	5
6–9	12
10–20	36
21–50	26
51 or more	7
No response	*

* Less than 0.5 percent.

TABLE 2-4

NUMBER OF MOVES IN LAST FIVE YEARS

Number of moves	Percent (N=623)
1	19
2	19
3	12
4 or more	12
None	30
Unusable responses[1]	7

1. The high number of unusable cases resulted, in large part, from our check on consistency between this question and an inquiry about length of residence at present address. Often the inconsistency seemed understandable, being due apparently to respondents thinking in terms of "about" five years.

This study, then, is interested in the effects of physical mobility on involvement patterns. Mobility seems to be obviously relevant. For instance, it would be understandable if as people separated spatially they lost interest in each other. Throughout this work we shall be interested in the relation between mobility and the distribution of involvement.

POVERTY   Table 2-7 presents the data on poverty. At the time of the study

TABLE 2–5

NUMBER OF DIFFERENT TOWNS AND CITIES LIVED IN

Number of Places	Percent (N=623)
1	16
2	39
3	21
4	10
Five or more	13
No response	1

TABLE 2–6

COMPOSITE OF MOBILITY VARIABLES

(Years at present address, number of moves in past five years, number of towns and cities lived in, length of time in Milwaukee, N=570[1])

Years at Present Address	Numbers of Moves in Last Five Years	Percent of Total Sample			
		Less than ten Years in Mil.		Ten or more Years in Mil.	
		Cosmopolitan[2]	Local[3]	Cosmopolitan	Local
	4 or more	2	6	2	3
One-four years	2–3	4	12	4	14
	1	2	8	2	9
Five-ten years	0	1	2	3	8
More than ten years	0	–	–	4	14

1. Unusable cases are not included in the table.

2. *Cosmopolitan* means that respondent has lived in 4 or more different towns and cities.

3. *Local* means that respondent has lived in 3 or less towns and cities.

TABLE 2-7

NUMBER OF RESPONDENTS BY FAMILY INCOME AND FAMILY SIZE[1]

(In parentheses are percentages based on those who answered income question)

Family Income Level	Family Size															Total
	1	2	3	4	5	6	7	8	9	10	11	12	13	14	15	
Below $1,000	29(6)	7(1)	4(1)	5(1)	4(1)	2*	1*	1*	1*							53
1,000–1,999	20(4)	28(6)	21(4)	11(2)	6(1)	4(1)	1*	1*	1*							94
2,000–2,999	13(3)	20(4)	12(3)	19(4)	9(2)	14(3)	5(1)	2*	2*	2*	2*					97
3,000–3,999	3(1)	17(4)	12(3)	8(2)	9(2)	13(3)	10(2)	11(2)	2*	1*	1*	1*	1*			91
4,000–4,999	2*	7(1)	5(1)	7(1)	7(1)	8(2)	7(1)	3(1)	7(1)	7(1)	2*	1*	1*			62
5,000–5,999	1*	2*	6(1)	5(1)	6(1)	3(1)	4(1)	1*	3(1)	1*	4(1)	1*	1*			38
6,000 and over	0	15(3)	12(3)	7(1)	8(2)	4(1)	2*	4(1)	5(1)	3(1)	2*	1*	1*			63
Refused to answer	12	26	13	5	9	4	5	3	1	1	1					80
Didn't know	2	4	4	1	2	0	1	0	2	1						18
No response	2	3	3	2	0	1	0	1								12
608[2] TOTAL	84	129	92	70	60	53	36	26	21	19	12	3	3			—

* Means less than .5%

1. Those within the staircase are by our minimal standards not poverty stricken; those above the staircase are poverty stricken; those below the staircase did not tell us their income.

2. The total is not 623, because the program that computed family size was performed when 15 cases were missing from our master tape; since there seemed to be no bias, we did not revise the table.

a common formula was to consider a family to be poverty-stricken if the family income was lower than the sum that would be arrived at by allowing $1,500 for the first person in the family and $500 for each person thereafter. A family of any size making $6,000 or more was not considered poverty-stricken. Our question about income was as follows: "Would you please look at this card and tell me which letter comes closest to your total family income before taxes for last year?" On the card handed to the respondent were a list of incomes in thousands of dollars, e.g., below $1,000, $1,000-$1,999, $2,000-$2,999, and so on . Since the responses were in intervals of a thousand, the aforementioned formula, which is based on intervals of 500, could not be used precisely. We chose to underestimate poverty, e.g., all families with four or fewer members and making $2,000-$2,999 are not considered poverty-stricken in this study; according to the formula using $500 intervals this would be true if the income were $2,999, but not if it were below $2,500; thus we have consistently underestimated poverty. For our female, homemaker sample, 41 percent of the households are poverty-stricken.[9]

Looking at the Table 2-7 it is once again the variety of situations that is impressive. To talk about 41 percent of the families being in poverty masks the variety of specific situations.

CONCLUSION

Kilbourntown lacks any unifying theme. There is the variety of buildings, with their different colors, sizes, shapes, conditions, and textures. And there is the variety of people-with their different colors, ages, socio-economic levels, and mobility patterns. Moreover, there is the steady stream of strangers either using the busy streets to go somewhere else or stopping temporarily at one of the non-neighborhood stores scattered about K-3. There is no obvious similarity unifying either the physical structure or the residents of Kilbourntown.

The types of establishments in the area do little to unify the neighborhood. There are the bars and churches, but these usually have a limited clientele; they are the homes for neighborhood cliques. Kilbourntown lacks the resources that would develop a multitude of casual contacts that would involve different people each day. For instance, there is no stroll street. Moreover, frequent moving from one residence to another make it unlikely that people of K-3 will develop high involvement relations with neighbors.

Our comments suggest that the physical environment plays an important role in shaping people's pattern of involvement. For instance, there is the possibly alienating effect of the variety of homes and of the poor distribution of trees. But the objection might be raised; what do we desire-"LEVITTOWN" with its repetitive and boring scenery? Perhaps disorder should be valued? But unity based on similarity does not require that objects be identical.

There is a form of unity that is aesthetical, as when objects of different sizes are all proportioned to each other. There is then a mathematical unity amid physical diversity.

Walking around Kilbourntown, one is struck by the lack of unity or harmony in the physical setting. This, in turn, leads to the thought that possibly harmony in the physical surroundings can contribute to the development of a sense of community, and to the theorem: positive involvement in face-to-face relations increases as does the aesthetic quality of the physical setting. The theorem is presented simply to suggest that there is a relation between aesthetics and a theory of involvement.

In succeeding chapters the relation between the "perceptual givens" of color and age and involvement will be examined, as well as the effects of mobility on involvement. In our analysis we examined the relation between income levels and various aspects of involvement. Little reference will be made to the results, because about all of them suggested that income level was insignificant. Because of the difficulty in getting accurate data on income through the use of questionnaires, we are not sure how to interpret these results.

3

Fantasy And Involvement

In Chapter One it was suggested that "the extent of involvement depends on the degree of overlap between the imaginary and sensed environments." The main point of this chapter is to examine the extent to which there is a lack of correspondence between the fantasy world and the sensed world among our respondents, and to suggest some reasons why there might not be correspondence.

There are at least two types of situations in which such correspondence would be absent: 1) when people think about objects that can not be seen or heard such as dead people or a deity; there are people who claim to have seen or heard spiritual beings; however, in our study it is assumed that our respondents who think about God or a dead person have not perceived or heard them; and 2) when people think about living individuals they rarely contact; it is assumed that during most of the time such living people are in fantasy, they will not simultaneously be part of the external sensed environment. Both types of situations will be discussed in this chapter.

We assume that to the extent the objects in a person's fantasy do not coincide with those in his sensed world, the individual will be alienated from his environment.

THE RELEVANT QUESTIONS ON THE QUESTIONNAIRE

There were two questions asked of the respondents that are relevant to the problem of fantasy. Both are open-ended and were meant to determine the most significant objects with which the respondent felt involved.

The first question is—"Who are the three people you think about most?"

We wanted a simple, concrete question that would reflect involvement, and that would not be biased by any preconceptions on our part. Thus, we did not inquire about people our respondents felt "close to," because this might have biased the responses in favor of people in the neighborhood. We assume that fantasy life mirrors "real" life, in the sense that the people thought about would be the most significant individuals in a persons's life. However, it must be clear that this question can be considered only a rough indication of involvement. It was hoped that although the question cannot precisely measure the degree of involvement the responses would indicate the persons with whom an individual is most involved.[1]

Questions were also asked about whether the imagined person was still alive, where the person lived, the relation of the person to the respondent, how frequently the respondent talked with the person named, and whether the respondent discussed personal problems with the individual thought about. These data will be used when appropriate.

A major weakness of the "think about" question is that it asks only about people: it is unable to find the individuals who relate to animals or who are most involved with a deity. Therefore, a second question was asked of the respondents—"What makes you feel proud?" If the respondent asked what was meant by this question the interviewer was instructed to add—"What would you tell people if you wanted to impress them?" The question was followed by five numbered blank lines. The study assumes that, if a person can feel proud about the actions or achievements of somebody or something else, he or she must be somehow involved in the source of pride. That is, the respondent must be a part of something to feel proud about it himself; we cannot feel anything about an object to which we are not related. Like the "think about" question, this inquiry about pride does not measure involvement precisely, it simply points out the objects in which a person is significantly involved; unlike our first question, however, the second is not limited to persons.[2]

THE DISTRIBUTION OF INVOLVEMENT

Before pursuing the question of the extent to which the respondents' fantasy does not reflect the sensed environment, it would be valuable to use the two open-ended questions to sketch out the respondents' overall pattern of involvement. Who are the people the homemakers of Kilbourntown think about? What are the respondents proud of?

THE "THINK ABOUT" QUESTION

In the original study the relation of the people "thought about" to the respondents was not determined. We attempted to reinterview about a 15 percent random sample of our respondents; this was done two months after the original study. In the reinterview specific questions were asked about the residential location of the persons thought about as well as the relation of these persons to the respondents. Of the 112 respondents we tried to recontact, 72 were interviewed; of the rest, 14 had definitely moved; the staff was not able to contact 24 respondents after three attempts. Of the 72 people reinterviewed, 63 were female homemakers. Obviously this subsample is biased in favor of the less mobile and more easily contacted part of the list of original respondents.

TABLE 3-1

FREQUENCY WITH WHICH DIFFERENT TYPES OF PEOPLE ARE THOUGHT ABOUT

(Listed as percentages)

	Age and color of respondent						
	17–39 years		*40–59 years*		*over 60*		*Total*
Type of person	*White (N=6)*	*Black (N=80)*	*White (N=21)*	*Black (N=44)*	*White (N=18)*	*Black (N=9)*	*(N=178)*
mother	17	23	5	14	6	11	16
father[1]	17	10		5		11	7
spouse		11	19	11	17	11	12
son[2]	17	16	29	7	22	11	16
daughter		13	38	9	28	22	16
"child"		3		2			2
brother		4		9			4
sister[3]		9	5	14	6	33	10
grandfather			5				1
grandmother							
granddaughter				2	6		1
grandson							
aunt		3					1
uncle							
niece		1		5	6		2
nephew				2			1
cousin				2			1
godmother			1				1
godfather							
friend		8		16	2		8
miscellaneous[4]	50			2			2

1. Includes one case of father-in-law.

2. Includes one case of son-in-law.

3. Includes three cases of sisters-in-law.

4. One person listed President and Mrs. Kennedy and a local judge; another referred to his landlord.

SOLIDARITY IN A SLUM

Table 3-1 shows the relation of the people thought about to the respondents for the subsample of 63 homemakers. Of the 178 people mentioned, all but 11 percent are members of each respondents' family. One striking characteristic of the fantasy world is that it is peopled by the family.

Considering the immediate family to be parents, spouse, children and siblings, 83 percent of the people thought about belonged to the immediate family. Moreover, 68 percent of these people are blood relatives. The significance of the family is not due to the importance of a single relationship; in fact as people age it seems that some family relationships replace others; so the importance of parents declines, while the significance of children and siblings increases. But our respondents do not go outside the family for fantasy figures. The specific relations change, but not the fact that they are familial relations. Even women living alone chose family members; five isolates chose fourteen people, twelve of whom were from their families. For the types of woman living in Kilbourntown, whether she is white or black, young or old, their fantasy life is an extension of family life, and if we are to understand what is happening on the fantasy level, we must study what is happening to the family in our society.

There is a difference, however, between whites and blacks. There are too few whites seventeen to thirty-nine years old to compare the two aggregates in this age range. But among those forty to fifty-nine years old there is a clear difference between whites and blacks; 86 percent of the people thought about by whites are members of the nuclear family, i.e., spouse, son, or daughter, while the comparable figure for blacks is 27 percent. Among those sixty and above the difference diminishes, but it is in the same direction; 66 percent of the whites' and 44 percent of the blacks' fantasy figures come from the nuclear family. Black involvement is diffused among members of the nuclear and extended family; white involvement is concentrated on the nuclear family. One result of this is that when black women meet, the probability is much higher for them than it is for white women that their patterns of involvement will be different. As a consequence it may be harder for black women to understand or to feel similar to each other. When white women meet, the shared topics of interest will no doubt be spouse and children. This will not be as true for black women. This phenomenon of diffused involvement seems especially true for the black women forty to fifty-nine years of age. Even friends are important for blacks in this age range; 16 percent of those thought about are friends, which is not very high, but it is the modal response.

Table 3-2 shows the distribution of responses on the "think about" question for the entire sample of 623 homemakers. Based on the subsample of 63 respondents who were reinterviewed, it can be assumed that category 8 in Table 3-2, "Person not child or spouse and not in home," refers mainly to members of the extended family. It would probably be correct, therefore, to combine categories 5 and 8.

TABLE 3–2

DISTRIBUTION OF RESPONSES TO "THINK ABOUT" QUESTION

Person thought about	Frequency mentioned			
	Response 1	Response 2	Response 3	Total
1. God	5	0	1	6
2. National political figures	7	5	1	13
3. Local political figures	0	0	1	1
4. Civil rights leaders	0	1	1	2
5. Religious Leaders	5	6	3	14
6. Self	8	1	1	10
7. Family reference	270	245	221	736
8. Person not child or spouse and not in home	262	259	214	735
9. Blank	66	106	180	352
	632	632	632	1869

But our interest in presenting Table 3-2 is to show the significance of recognizably nonfamilial persons (categories 1-5) in the fantasy life of our respondents. No nonfamilial category was mentioned by more than 2 percent of the sample. The overriding fact remains that fantasy seems to reflect family.

Religion and politics, however, do enter into the fantasy life of Kilbourntown. Considering that the question asked about "three people" the respondent thought about, it is remarkable that six people did mention God. Although some individuals think of God as an idea, similar to an abstraction like "equality," many people tend to think of God as a person to whom they can relate. God is someone to love, fear, or worship. God is a source of comfort and command. God to most people is not an abstraction but a person and as such is a part of the personal world of the respondents. We shall return to this topic.

Not only is God important but so is the religious institution. Fourteen religious leaders are thought about.

We could only identify this category if the respondent used either "Father" or "Reverend" in naming the person; it is quite possible that in coding we missed some religious leaders who were named but for whom no religious title was given. Thirteen of the fourteen references to religious leaders were made by black people. The relative importance of religion to black people will be a recurrent theme in this work. Again, we shall return to this topic. For now, it is sufficient to emphasize the point that the homemakers of Kilbourntown, or at least some of them, extend their involvement beyond the family to God and church.

SOLIDARITY IN A SLUM

Seemingly of about equal importance with the religious institution is politics. One striking fact, however, is the absence of local political leaders. Political involvement seems to occur only on the national level. In part this reflects that truly memorable people, charismatic people, are able to make it to the top of the political ladder. So several respondents mentioned Mr. and Mrs. John F.Kennedy, and one even mentioned Franklin Delano Roosevelt. These were politicians who literally captured the imagination of the people. But Lyndon B. Johnson, president at the time of the study, was also mentioned; his existence in our respondent's fantasy would not seem due to his charismatic qualities but to the importance of the presidential office for the residents of Kilbourntown.

The almost complete absence of reference to civil rights leaders, national or local, was quite surprising. The "think about" question followed a series of inquiries about voluntary associations; one of these queries specifically asked about membership in civil rights groups, so that the respondents were reminded of this category almost immediately before answering the "think about" question. Of course our sample is mainly from the lower class, but the ratio of political leaders to civil rights leaders seems important. Given the fact that political leaders were mentioned, the near absence of reference to civil rights leaders indicates how little this movement had penetrated the black masses at the time of the study.

Ten people mentioned themselves in response to the "think about" question. This is a small number, but it points to an aspect of involvement not touched on yet in this work. A study in depth might indeed reveal that self-involvement is the most wide-spread form of involvement. As with the reference to God, it is surprising that in response to the "think about" question anyone would mention themselves.

What, then, is the pattern of involvement suggested by the "think about" question? Assuming that what is mentioned by a minority of respondents is on the periphery of involvement for the majority, the following picture emerges: a concentration of involvement on the family, with a modest degree of involvement in God, church, country, and self. But the "think about" question is of limited use, since it refers only to specific persons. It is not very useful, therefore, for measuring involvement in organizations or abstractions like "equality". Let us compare the conclusion drawn from the "think about" question, therefore, with the responses to the "proud" question. The exact wording of the latter was simply—"What makes you feel proud?" It is regretable that we did not, also, ask our respondents what makes them feel ashamed. The "proud" question reflects only positive involvement. One of the virtues of the "think about" question is that it can indicate either positive or negative involvement, people loved as well as people hated.

Table 3-3 shows the distribution of responses to the "proud" question. As compared with the "think about" question (see Table 3-2), the responses to the "proud" question are less concentrated. This is no doubt due to the greater openness of the "proud" question; quite literally, it allows people to mention anything.

There is no change, however, in the dominance of the family, which remains the modal response. It occurs twice as often as the next most frequent category. Within the family category references are scattered over a variety of family roles, though clearly children are the most frequent family member the respondents are proud of. In fact, the percentage of references to children, 15 percent, is the highest percentage given any single subcategory. Perhaps it is only lower-class people who take so much pride in their children, perhaps in part as consolation for their own frustrations. It would be valuable to have comparable studies of middle-and upper-class neighborhoods in order to determine the relative significance of the 15 percent figure. In the next chapter the parent-child relationship will be examined in more detail.

TABLE 3–3

DISTRIBUTION OF RESPONSES TO THE "PROUD" QUESTION

(Percentages based on total number of responses actually given.)

Object proud about		Percent of total responses (N=1136)	
1. Physical things (e.g., cars, flowers)		5	
2. Animals		(N=6, or less than .5%)	
3. Country or president		11	
4. Freedom or tolerance in U.S.		5	18
5. Educational opportunities now available		1	
6. War in Vietnam		1	
7. Milwaukee		1	
8. Racial reference		1	
9. Nonracial ethnic reference		1	
10. Reference to church or specific religion		2	7
11. Reference to personal religious practices or to God		5	
12. References to family		36	
spouse	7		
children	15		
parents	4		
other	10		
13. Self		20	
Personal achievements[1]	12		
Health	5		
To be alive	3		
14. Job		2	
15. Friends		1	
16. Miscellaneous		7	

1. Includes references to abilities and favourable personality traits (e.g., kindness).

The significance of political involvement as indicated by the "proud" questions is surprising. If items 2 through 6 in Table 3-3 are considered in their relation to national politics, then 18 percent of the responses indicated national political involvement. The rarity of references to Milwaukee matches the almost complete absence of local political leaders in the responses to the "think about" question. Political involvement for the homemakers of K-3 means only national political involvement.

But what is to be made of the greater significance of politics over religion, to which only 7 percent of the responses refer? This difference can probably be explained by the context in which the "proud" question was asked. It followed a series of questions intended to measure national involvement. The immediately preceding question was—"Do you agree or disagree that people who refuse to fight for their country when it is in trouble should not be allowed to live in that country?" Seven such questions preceded the proud question. That 18 percent of the responses to the "proud" question related to national concern was in part the result of the context in which the question was asked. On the other hand there were no references in these preceding questions to freedom, tolerance, or educational opportunities, which were mentioned in 6 percent of the responses to the "proud" question. Of course, the preceding questions made political events in general salient. But the references to such things as freedom and tolerance suggest a genuine and positive involvement with the country. However, the difference between the percentage for country and for religion is no doubt exaggerated due to the nature of the preceding questions.

That only 1 percent of the sample referred to race as a source of pride indicates that at the time of this study there was little sense of positive racial identity that could serve as a basis for a racial social movement. There were more references (5 percent) to the ideological catchwords of such a movement —such as freedom and equality. Remember that interviewers generally were of the same color as those interviewed; still, race remained unimportant. It could be, of course, that the respondents are more ashamed of their color than proud of it. It could also be that color is significant at a pre-conscious level and so is not thought of in response to an open-ended question. Moreover, there is the fact that the questionnaire was administered in the respondent's house, where the family was salient. But this last point does not seem to adequately explain the scarcity of references to race; for on the "think about" question many family members were named who did not live with the respondent, and on the "proud" question a majority of the responses did not refer to the family. At least at the time of this study (Spring, 1966) race did not seem to be an important source of self-identity for our respondents.

Similarly, work is not an important source of pride. About 13 percent (eighty-six) of the women in the sample said that their own job was the main source of family income; 2 percent of the responses to the "proud" question relate to our respondents' jobs. It is reasonable to assume that in light of the unattractive jobs the respondents are likely to have, it is amazing that even 2 percent of the responses refer to their work.

Friends also fall into the class of unimportant objects. Both the "think about" and the "proud" question reveal a huge gulf between family and friends. That the family is more important than friends in the lower class is not surprising, but the degree of difference makes us pause.

Consistent with the "think about" results, religion is a significant category for the "proud" question. But only a total of 23 people mentioned a specific religion or church. As will be discussed in Chapter Five, our respondents do go to church, but this affiliation is of only modest importance. The fact that more references are given to personal religious practices or to the personal relation to a deity suggests that for our sample the spiritual relationship is more important than the social relations that are a consequence of church affiliation itself.

The "self" is more significant on the "proud" question than it was on the "think about." In part this resulted from our respondents' interest in health. There is a consistent, positive relation between age and references to health; as people age they become concerned about health and proud of good health, if they are fortunate enough to have it. One consequence of the increase in concern about health, which is related to age, is that it means greater self-involvement as people become older.

The pride the respondents took in physical things should probably be considered as self-pride. A car, for instance, is often a status symbol and reflects the success of the owner. To be proud of one's flower garden is likewise to be proud of one's own achievement. It would be correct, therefore, to add together items 1 and 13, which would mean that a total of 25 percent of the references involve the self. At least to this writer this rather high percentage is surprising. One tends to associate slum areas with an absence of self-respect based on individual accomplishments. But, clearly, such self-respect exists to a significant degree in Kilbourntown.

It might be thought that Table 3-3 does not adequately reflect the relative importance of the different categories. After all it is easier to say more than one thing about some objects than others; for instance, it might be easier to list more items under family than under job. To hold constant the number of references per category, Table 3-4 shows the distribution of responses using only the first response given by the respondents. As can be seen, the results in Tables 3-3 and 3-4 are almost identical. Regarding the relative importance of different categories our comments based on Table 3-3 need no revision.

However, Table 3-4 makes an additional point. If we assume that the first response indicates what is most important to the respondent, then the results in Table 3-4 reveal a diversity of involvement patterns in Kilbourntown. For a third of the respondents the family comes first, but about a fifth begin with the country (but remember the influence of questionnaire context) and another fifth with the self. Slightly less than 10 percent begin with religion, and the rest are scattered. In a sense there are four different types of involvement patterns based on the four different starting points: family, country, self, and religion. No doubt each gives rise to a unique perspective on the world.

Tables 3-1 through 3-4, then, present a generally consistent picture of the respondents' patterns of involvement. Dominant is the family, although for whites this means the nuclear family, while for blacks it refers to the extended

TABLE 3-4

DISTRIBUTION OF FIRST RESPONSES TO THE "PROUD" QUESTION

(Percentages based on number of responses actually given.)

Object proud about	Percent of response (N=495)	
1. Physical things (e.g., car, flowers)	3%	
2. Animals	*	
3. Country or president	16	
4. Freedom or tolerance in U.S.	5	
5. Educational opportunities now available	1	23%
6. War in Vietnam	1	
7. Milwaukee	1	
8. Racial reference	2	
9. Nonracial ethnic reference	1	
10. Reference to church or specific religion	3	
11. Reference to personal religious practices or to God	5	8
12. Reference to family	35	
spouse	(7)[1]	
children	(17)	
parents	(2)	
other	(9)	
13. Self	20	
Personal achievement	(9)[2]	
Health	(7)	
To be alive	(4)	
14. Job	1	
15. Friends	0	
16. Miscellaneous	6	

* Only one respondent said she was proud of her pet.

1. The percentages in brackets are breakdowns of the major categories. So, seven percent of the total sample said they are proud of their spouse.

2. I.e., nine percent said they are proud of their personal achievements, which we classified as indicating self-pride.

family. Secondary foci for involvement are the self, the country, and religion. But there are some individuals for whom each of these secondary foci will be of primary importance. Racial or ethnic collectivities, work, friends, voluntary associations other than churches—all these seem to be of little importance. In subsequent chapters we shall further explore respondents' involvement in the family, religion, and country. We did not anticipate the importance of self-involvement; the failure to investigate this area is a serious gap in this study.

THE ABSENCE OF INVOLVEMENT

In discussing the "distribution of involvement" we considered actual responses to the "think about" and "proud" questions. But what about the blanks?

Blanks for open-ended questions are difficult to evaluate because this type of question is so demanding of the interviewer. Giving only one or two responses to the "think about" question might simply mean that the interviewer did not urge the respondent to give three answers or that the interviewer did not allow sufficient time for a third name to occur to the person being interviewed. Blanks might not tell us anything about the subject's fantasy life; they might simply reflect the interviewer's inadequacy. In an attempt to determine the significance of interviewing skills, interviewers were compared in terms of their effectiveness in eliciting responses to the "think about" question. There was quite a range of success in getting "think about" responses, but one interviewer was clearly poorer that all the rest. In sixteen out of twenty-nine cases she had no responses; this was the only interviewer who failed more than she succeeded. Her interviews are excluded from the analysis in this section. It seems undeniable, however, that to some unknown extent the presence of blanks is due to the conditions of the interview experience itself, and not to the nature of our respondents' fantasy life.

It could be argued that the presence of blanks might simply indicate difficulty in understanding the question. To check this we determined the number of blanks by age and education; there are some differences in the expected direction, i.e., the more educated had fewer blanks, but the range of the differences is not great, and the apparent effect of education differed among age aggregates; among those forty to sixty-nine years old the range across educational levels was 11 percent, while among those sixty and above the range was 1 percent. The difference did not seem sufficient to warrant further consideration of the education variable.

Some people gave collective-type responses to the "think about" question, e.g., "family," or "the children." It might be thought that such people would have more blanks. In fact the opposite was true; the 43 people who gave this type of response had a total of 5 percent blank responses; those individuals who gave at least one response of any type (N=558) had a total of 9 percent blank responses.

Since the "think about" question is used as an indicator of involvement, it might be proposed that blanks would mean an absence of involvement. But that would be inaccurate. Singer studied a "sample of 240, presumably normal, adults between the ages 19 and 50, of at least college education, who came from a fairly widespread area in the United States...." He found that "96% of the respondents reported that they engaged in some form of daydreaming daily. ..."[3] But—"The maximum daydreaming reported is between the ages eighteen and twenty-nine, with decreasing frequency in the thirty to thirty-nine group, and with lowest reported frequency in persons aged forty to forty-nine."[4] Although Singer's sample is quite different from ours, the fact that 96 percent of his respondents reported at least daily daydreaming suggests that all humans have some sort of meaningful fantasy life. Therefore, if people cannot name three people they think about, this cannot be assumed to indicate an absence or paucity of fantasy but only that the fantasy activity is not diffused among at least three *real* people. Actually there are two dimensions to consider: 1) fantasy may be focused or diffused, i.e., limited to a few or involving new people continually, and 2) fantasy may be about real or imaginary people. An inability to name three people in response to the "think about" question could occur, therefore, for the following reasons: a) the person's involvement is so diffused that it is difficult to pick out one, two, or three specific people, or b) the person's fantasy is mainly about imaginary people, or c) the person has no fantasy. According to Singer, "c" becomes more possible as people age; this might indicate a general decline of activity, and therefore, of involvement—in short, disengagement. Condition "b" would mean a lack of correspondence between fantasy life and social life, and therefore alienation. Condition "a"—a diffused fantasy—would seem to mean the absence of deep involvement—a flighty person. It is assumed, therefore, that blanks on the "think about" indicate alienation, although there are three possible reasons.

For the total sample, whites and blacks have almost identical percentages of blank responses to the "think about" question: 15 percent for the whites, 16 percent for the blacks. Even holding age constant, there are no dramatic differences between the color aggregates, the largest difference being 6 percent for those forty to forty-nine years old. Table 3-5 presents the percentage of blank responses to the "think about" question by age. The two extreme aggregates obviously deviate from the other age ranges, but the subsamples at the extremes are quite small.

As noted in the last chapter we are especially interested in the impact of mobility on involvement. Accordingly, the percentage of blanks was related to number of cities lived in, years at present address, and years in Milwaukee. By and large no pattern emerged except for those forty to fifty-nine years old, and this pattern remained regardless of household size. Table 3-6 shows the relation between the percentage of blanks and years in Milwaukee for people in

TABLE 3–5

PERCENT OF BLANK RESPONSES TO THE "THINK" ABOUT QUESTION

(By age of respondent, N=590[1])

Age in years	Percent blank	
	%	N
17–19	2	(15)
20–29	14	(147)
30–39	17	(148)
40–49	17	(101)
50–59	17	(67)
60–74	13	(82)
75–98	23	(20)
No response		(10)

1. This is our total after we removed the interviews conducted by the inadequate interviewer noted in the text. There were twenty nine interviews done by this interviewer; we also removed two other cases in which the interviewer was not identified; finally two cases were eliminated because of coding errors.

this age range who are not lifetime residents of Milwaukee. There is a curvilinear relationship (i.e., one where the relationship between the variables changes as the values change) between the percentage and the number of years in Milwaukee. But why would those mobile people who have lived eleven to twenty-five years in Milwaukee have a high percentage of blanks? If mobility

TABLE 3–6

PERCENT OF BLANKS ON THE "THINK ABOUT" QUESTION RELATIVE TO YEARS SPENT IN MILWAUKEE: AMONG THOSE WHO HAVE LIVED IN MORE THAN ONE CITY AND WHO ARE FORTY TO FIFTY-NINE YEARS OLD

Years in Milwaukee	Percent blank	
	%	N
0–5		(11)
6–10	12	(22)
11–15	27	(27)
16–20	30	(23)
21–25	23	(22)
26–55	2	(32)
[Lifetime residents	11	(21)]

itself is significant, the high percentage would have been expected among the newcomers to Milwaukee. Of course it is possible that it takes around ten years for people to forget those with whom they were significantly involved; this seems difficult to believe, yet it is a possibility. But, then, why does it take ten to fifteen years more to replace lost relationships and thus for the percentage to go down? It could be that it actually takes about ten years to feel so involved with someone that respondents would mention them in response to the "think about"question. This seems absurd in regard to a spouse, but perhaps there is some value in looking more closely into the time dimension of involvement. How long does it take to develop a deep involvement with someone? No doubt the answer is related to the significance attributed to a relationship by culture. In the United States great significance, and therefore power, is given to one's spouse, and thus he or she is likely to be thought about frequently soon after the marital relation begins. But American culture is vague about the significance of other relations, and perhaps it does take considerable time for people, even family members (other than spouses), to develop a deep involvement.

But it could also be that mobility itself is not important, and that the results in Table 3-6 are due to the effect of another, unknown variable. There were too few cases in some of the subsamples to do an analysis for those below forty. However, there was no indication of any relation between years in Milwaukee and percentage of blanks for those sixty and above. At best, then we can say that there is weak support for the idea that there is a curvilinear relation between the length of residence in a city and the percentage of blanks.

Litwak has already suggested that mobility does not undermine family involvement, so the absence of a relationship between mobility and blanks should not surprise us. Moreover, the studies of Brown et al. and Tilly and Brown have shown the importance of kin in the migration process. Speaking of migrants, Tilly and Brown wrote: "Everywhere we find more persistence and proliferation of personal relations than should be there. The very groups one would expect to find disrupted by migration, for lack of security, experience or skill in city life, show extensive contacts among kinfolk." Clearly, our finding that mobility does not seem to diminish familial involvement is supported by other studies.[5]

TYPES OF INVOLVEMENT THAT PRODUCE ALIENATION

Earlier in the chapter the point was made that involvement with certain objects is itself a source of alienation, since when those objects are thought about, the resulting fantasies cannot simply reflect in mirror-like fashion the sensed environment. To what extent were the respondents involved with such objects?

TABLE 3–7

PERCENT OF RESPONDENTS REFERRING TO DEITY ON "PROUD" QUESTION

(By age and color of respondent)

	Color	
Age	White	Black
17–19	(3)	(11)
20–39	3 (36)	6 (245)
40–59	5 (59)	15 (103)
60–74	2 (48)	34 (38)
75–98	5 (20)	(2)
No response	(3)	(8)

DEITY

One indicator of involvement in the deity is whether or not the respondent mentioned God as one of the three people thought about. Six people did mention God. Of course, this underestimates the significance of spiritual relations, because people do not usually think of God as simply "a person." Another indicator of involvement with the deity is whether or not people mentioned their personal religious practices or their relation to God as something they are proud of. If they did, significant spiritual involvement can be assumed. However, if people fail to mention God this does not necessarily mean the absence of spiritual involvement; it may mean that the respondent does not value her spiritual relationship as much as other aspects of her life. In spite of this, we will use the "proud" question in the discussion of spiritual involvement. The reader must bear in mind, however, that this question reflects not simply involvement, but valued involvement.

In analyzing the proud question we differentiated between responses that referred to specific churches or religious organizations and those that referred either to personal religious practices, such as praying, or to a relationship with a deity; it is the latter type of response in which we are interested. The deity (i.e., the relationship to a deity) was mentioned by fifty-seven respondents (9 percent of our sample). Table 3-7 shows the distribution of these references by age and color. Observably, pride in one's relationship to the deity is a black phenomenon in Kilbourntown; more precisely, it exists mainly among the older blacks.[6]

Marx has recently compared the religiosity of blacks and whites.

There is a popular stereotype that Negroes are a 'religious people.' Social science research has shown that they are 'over-churched' relative to whites, i.e., the ratio of Negro churches to the size of the Negro population is greater than the same ratio for whites. Using data from a nationwide survey of whites, by Gertrude Selznick and Stephan Steinberg, some comparison of the religiosity of Negroes and whites was possible. When these various dimensions of religiosity were examimed, with effect of education and region held constant, Negroes appeared as significantly more religious only with respect to the subjective importance assigned to religion. In the north, whites were more likely to attend church at least once a week than were Negroes; while in the South rates of attendance were the same. About the same percentage of both groups had no doubts about the existence of God. While Negroes were more likely to be sure about the existence of a devil, whites, surprisingly, were more likely to be sure about a life beyond death. Clearly, then, any assertions about the greater religiosity of Negroes relative to whites are unwarranted unless one specifies the dimension of religiosity.[7]

Our research does support the "popular stereotype" that Negroes are "a religious people." At least between the whites and blacks dwelling together in an urban slum there is a clear difference regarding the deity. Blacks value the spiritual relationships in which they are involved; whites do not, either because they are not involved in spiritual relationships or because they do not value such involvements.[8]

If sociologists and others are to understand people they must clearly recognize the distinction between spiritual involvement and institutional (or church) involvement. More people in our sample referred to the former than the latter. Deities are people, or at least that is how they are considered by the majority of believers. God is not an idea, an abstraction, a belief—but a person. Jesus Christ, for instance, might be related to as a lover, a father, a friend, a helper, and so on—only he is a superlover, a superfather, a superfriend.

But spiritual involvement, precisely because it is a humanlike relationship, can be a source of alienation from our fellow man. It has already been pointed out that involvement with a deity produces alienation, because it cuts off our fantasy from the sensed environment. But spiritual involvement can alienate us in still another way. Because the Christian God is a superfather or a superfriend or a super-whatever, he can take the place of purely human counterparts. Because God is humanlike he can turn people away from involvement with the humans about them. The Christian image of God must be a great temptation leading believers to turn away from the purely human. It might be argued that, on the contrary, being a Christian leads to involvement in human affairs; for instance, it might inspire crusades for social justice. Note, however, that our discussion is not about "being a Christian" but about being involved with a deity. Someone might actively support Christian morality but give little attention to the person of God. But it is the latter on which we are commenting. The blacks of Kilbourntown, more than the whites, seemed involved with God. Possibly, this means not only that fantasy cannot mirror the sensed environment, but also that black women may turn away from human relations for the perfection of the Christian God.

But the involvement with the deity is not equally important for all black women. Rather its importance increases with age. Given the fact that approaching death does not make the elderly white women more religious, it would seem hazardous to suggest that the difference between the younger and older black women is due to the effects of different life stages. It is possible that this difference reflects generational change, i.e., perhaps the older black women have failed to pass on the value of spiritual involvement. However, it cannot be forgotten that the proud question is open-ended. Perhaps for young black women it is not that they are not involved with God, or that they do not value this involvement, but that other things such as family and children are more salient, so that they forgot about God, for awhile. Fully one-third of the older black women refered to a spiritual relationship, and it must be remembered that open-ended questions underestimate the prevalence of relationships. For older black women in Kilbourntown alienation due to involvement in a spiritual relationship would seem quite significant. It must be very hard for nonbelievers or for those whose religion is mainly a matter of morality to understand the way in which these older black women experience the world.

THE DEAD

For a discussion of the last two types of objects—dead persons and persons rarely contacted—we return to the "think about" question.

The prominence of the dead at least in some primitive societies is well known.

> It is not enough to state that the dead are constantly present to the minds of the living, who do nothing without consulting them; that the well-being, prosperity and very existence of the social group depend upon the good will of its dead members, and that these in their turn cannot dispense with the worship and the offerings of their descendants. The solidarity existing between them is yet more profound and more intimate, and it is realized in the very essence of individuals. The dead 'live with' the members of their group who are born into the world.[9]

Compared to most, if not all, primitive societies, the dead play a minor role in American society. The modern mythology is future-oriented, and so pays little homage to past commoners or heroes. If anything, our society seems to worship the young. Despite this dramatic change on the mythological level, however, the dead remain important to many modern people. For whom are the dead important? Which dead linger on in our social world? These are the questions we are presently interested in.

The "think about" question asked our 623 respondents to name three

TABLE 3–8

PERCENT OF REFERENCES TO PEOPLE WHO ARE DEAD ON THE
"THINK ABOUT" QUESTION

	(By age of respondent)		
Age	Percent of references		Percent of respondents who think about at least one dead person
	%	N	%
17–19	0	(15)	0
20–29	2	(156)	5
30–39	3	(156)	9
40–49	5	(104)	12
50–59	5	(71)	10
60–74	7	(88)	11
75–98	18	(22)	27
No response		(11)	—

people, implying a possibility of 1,869 different replies. However, only 1,520 choices were actually made. Of the actual replies 81, or a little over 5 percent are dead. Of the 623 respondents, 40 chose one dead person, 16 chose two, and 3 gave three dead persons; in short, about 9 percent of our sample mentioned at least one dead person in response to the "think about" question. The deceased are a minor, but noteworthy part of the social world even in urban America, although this characteristic might be restricted to the urban slum.

Who are these remembered dead? As noted previously, we attempted to reinterview about a 15 percent random sample of our respondents. The sixty-three female homemakers reinterviewed had mentioned 177 persons on the "think about" question, 13 of whom were dead (i.e., about 7 percent). Their relations to our respondents were as follows: Mother—5; spouse—2; sister—1; aunt—1; daughter—1; grandfather—1; friend—1; President Kennedy—1.

WHO THINKS ABOUT DEAD PEOPLE?

Table 3-8 presents data relating age to thinking about the dead. Although this phenomenon begins early in life, it obviously also increases with age. The percentages in the first column of this table are based on the total number of possible responses; if only the total number of actual responses is considered, i.e., if blanks are excluded, the percentages are: 0, 2, 4, 6, 7, and 23. Of those people mentioned by respondents over seventy-four, just about one-fourth are dead. A comparison of whites and blacks by age-aggregate showed no significant differences.

TABLE 3–9

PERCENT OF RESPONDENTS WHO THINK ABOUT AT LEAST
ONE DEAD PERSON

(By marital status[1] of respondent)

Marital status	Percent	
	%	N
Never married	10	(19)
Married	9	(360)
Divorced	11	(37)
Separated	5	(97)
Widowed	16	(80)
No response		(5)

1. N=608, because this analysis was done subdividing marital status by household size, and we
have data on household size for only 608 cases.

In table 3-8 the data are presented in two ways—as a percentage of all
the references that were to persons who were dead and as the percentage of
respondents who thought about at least one dead person. The overall pattern
is the same in both cases. To know that, at least for this lower-class sample
of women, one-quarter of the elderly are significantly involved with the dead
may help the rest of the population understand the perspective of those near
the death side of life.

In an attempt to explore further who thinks about the dead, this type of
involvement was related to marital status (see Table 3-9). As expected, widows
have the highest percentage. But this could be due to the fact that having lost
a spouse, they have a dead person with whom they were significantly involved
while he was alive to think about. In fact, being a widow is associated with
thinking about the dead only if the widow was fifty or more; none of the sixteen
widows younger than this thought about the dead. On the other hand, for each
age-aggregate fifty and over (i.e., fifty to fifty-nine, sixty to seventy-four,
seventy-five to ninety-eight) at least 20 percent of the widows think about at
least one dead person. Although the subsamples are small it does seem that
there is nothing in widowhood itself that makes people think about the dead.
It is far from automatic for a widow to continue being deeply involved with
her spouse after he dies, especially if the widow is young.

However, this study did not gather data on how recent was the spouse's
death and this is probably important. Townsend and Tunstall concluded from
their cross-cultural study of old people: "Loneliness is related much more to
'loss' than to enduring 'isolation'. There is evidence not only that the recently

widowed are more likely to be extremely lonely than those widowed for many years, but also that persons whose children die or who have become separated from their children, and persons who have been detached in other ways from their social circle (such as people who are moved into a house or flat in a new district), feel lonely."[10] It seems quite possible that a recent loss will have different effects from a distant one. Perhaps the percent of recent widows thinking about dead people would be quite high.

It is interesting that 'separated' women have an unusually low percentage in Table 3-9. This remained true for all age categories (data not shown). Perhaps the fact that some people separate rather than divorce indicates a casualness about social relations in general. Perhaps separated people are more flexible and find it easier to change involvements. This casualness need not mean shallow relationships. Theoretically, a person may feel very involved with another but also may easily give up that involvement and become involved with another person. It would be valuable to determine if, in fact, people can be flexibly yet deeply involved. A study of separated persons might be especially fruitful if one was interested in this question.

PEOPLE RARELY TALKED WITH

The respondents were asked how often they talked with the people they think about. The response categories used were: daily, several times a week, once a week, two or three times a month, or less than two or three times a month. We are here interested in the last category, i.e., the people our respondents talk with once a month or less; about 15 percent of the possible responses are people rarely talked with. To fantasize about people rarely seen or heard is to contribute to the separation of the fantasy world from the sensed world, and, therefore, to increase alienation.

Neither age nor color shows any consistent relation to thinking about individuals rarely talked with. Table 3-10 shows the percentage of the fantasy world given over to people rarely talked with by age and color. Two slight tendencies are noticeable, namely that blacks consistently have slightly higher percentages and that the peak period is in the thirty to thirty-nine year age-range.

Mobility is important in understanding why people fantasize about individuals with whom they rarely communicate; only 5 of the 274 people the respondents rarely talked with came from the neighborhood; it is because people move about that our sample now had relations with individuals they rarely got to talk to. For the subsample we reinterviewed about the people they think about, there were thirty cases of people rarely contacted; only four of these people then lived in Milwaukee; the rest lived in Tennessee, Chicago, Arkansas, Mississippi, and California. In their fantasy world the people of K-3

TABLE 3–10

PERCENT OF RESPONSES REFERRING TO PEOPLE WITH WHOM THE RESPONDENT IS RARELY IN CONTACT

(By age and color of respondent)

Age	Color			
	White		Black	
	%	N	%	N
17–19		(3)		(11)
20–29		(11)	13	(134)
30–39	15	(25)	20	(112)
40–49	6	(26)	15	(69)
50–59	10	(33)	17	(34)
60–74	12	(48)	17	(38)
75 and over	8	(20)		(2)
No response		(3)		(8)

are in contact with all parts of this nation. They can not be completely provincial. This scattering of relations reflects the mobility of the American population in general.

As would be expected the more stable respondents tended to think about people with whom they are in frequent contact. For the sixty-one respondents who have lived in Milwaukee all their life,[11] only 6 percent of their possible responses to the "think about" question are individuals rarely talked with; this is half the percentage for the total sample. We also considered the length of time our respondents lived at their present address; almost all of our respondents (95 percent) under thirty had lived at their present address no more than five years; obviously, length of residence could not differentiate among them. Even among those in their thirties only 5 percent had lived in their present house more than ten years. For those in their forties and fifties, longer residence in the same house is associated with a decline in the number of references to people rarely talked with; for both age-aggregates those living at the same address more than ten years show this decline. On the other hand, those over sixty seem unaffected by length of residence. In general then, more stable people think less about people they rarely communicate with. But the degree to which this source of alienation is present reflects the mobility patterns not only of our respondents, but also the patterns of potential fantasy objects, i.e., of family members. Our respondents' stability, then, could be expected to explain only a part of the tendency to think about people rarely contacted.

SUMMARY ANALYSIS OF "THINK ABOUT" QUESTION

To get some idea of the overall degree to which respondents are involved in their sensed environment, Table 3-11 is presented. The "think about" question was used to measure: a) the absence of significant involvement (percentage of blanks), and b) the presence of involvement with objects that produce some degree of alienation because fantasy will not mirror the sensed environment (percentage of persons thought about who are dead; percentage of persons thought about who are rarely contacted). If we combine all three percentages and subtract from 100 percent we get a measure of the extent to which respondents are involved with the sensed environment. The measure of involvement is shown in the parentheses in Table 3-11.

The only subcategory that stands out is that of persons seventy-five and over; clearly, they are low in their involvement; this seems to result both from a high percentage of blanks and from relatively frequent reference to dead people. In short, the "disengagement" of the old may reflect both a decline in involvement and a shift of involvement from the living to the dead.

The major difference by color concerns spiritual involvement, and this is

TABLE 3–11

PERCENT OF RESPONSES ON THE "THINK ABOUT" QUESTION THAT
ARE BLANK OR THAT REFER TO THE DEAD OR TO THE RARELY
TALKED WITH BY AGE AND COLOR

(The figure in parentheses is 100 minus the total.)

	White				Black			
Age	Blank[1]	Dead	Rarely talked with	Total	Blank[1]	Dead	Rarely talked with	Total
17–19[2]	—	—	—	—	(11)	—	—	—
20–29[3]	—	—	—	—	15%	1%	13%	29%(71)
30–39	12%	7%	15%	34%(66)	17	3	20	40 (60)
40–49	12	5	6	23 (77)	18	5	15	38 (62)
50–59	18	3	10	31 (69)	18	5	17	40 (60)
60–74	16	8	12	36 (64)	11	4	17	32 (68)
75–98[4]	24	18	8	50 (50)	(2)	—	—	—

1. Percentages in this column are based on our total sample minus the cases obtained by the inadequate interviewer. We have assumed that the figures would have been the same if the entire sample had been adequately interviewed.

2. There are too few cases to justify analysis.

3. There are too few white respondents to justify analysis.

4. There are too few black respondents to justify analysis.

not reflected in Table 3-11. If we could somehow combine a measure of this variable with the others contained in this table, there would probably be a significant difference between whites and blacks, with the latter being more alienated from the sensed environment.

CONCLUSION

The point of this chapter has been to develop an understanding of alienation resulting from a divergence between fantasy and the sensed environment. We have tried to show the extent to which such alienation exists among our respondents.

But, it is one thing to lay bare the basis for objective alienation and another thing to claim that people actually experience this alienation as such. What Cortazar says about "metaphysical rivers" is meant to apply to life in general: "There are metaphysical rivers, she swims in them like that swallow swimming in the air, spinning madly around a belfry, letting herself drop so that she can rise up all the better with the swoop. I describe and define and desire those rivers, but she swims in them. I look for them, find them, observe them from the bridge, but she swims in them."[12] Sociologists are the definers, observers. But the people we study swim in reality. Scientists stand back, people dive in. It would be quite erroneous to assume that all objective alienation is simultaneously subjective alienation.

Kornhauser, among others, has suggested that the United States be considered a "mass society," one which is characterized by "(1) the weakness of intermediary relations [i.e., the local community, local press, voluntary organizations, the work group], (2) the isolation of primary relations, (3) the centralization of national relations."[13] The distribution of involvement found among our respondents is somewhat consistent with this model. Most intermediary institutions are unimportant—however, with the strong exception of the religious institution. The importance of this institution calls into question the relevance of the "mass society" model to our respondents. On the other hand, consistent with this model is the unimportance of local politics and the concentration of political involvement on the national level. But a final evaluation of this model awaits a clearer specification of what "the isolation of primary relations" means. In the meanwhile it seems to me that the importance our respondents attached to the family seriously questions the appropriateness of the label 'mass society." Family and religion are important sources of counterpressures for whatever forces are generated by the state. The model of a "mass society" is useful but cannot adequately express the richness of social life in Kilbourntown.

4

The Household and Family

Several ideas set forth in Chapter One are important for understanding our perspective on the household. For women, and especially housewives, there are probably only two universally important environments—fantasy and the household. The first question we ask, therefore, is how much overlap is there between our respondents' fantasy world and household? This represents a refinement of the analysis presented in the previous chapter.

Second, and the major topic of this chapter, we want to know some details about the pattern of familial involvement in Kilbourntown. Are wives always deeply involved with their husbands? Are mothers equally involved with all children? How does color and age affect the pattern of involvement? In this chapter we shall try to delve deeper into what the data in the last chapter suggested was the central object in our respondents' lives—their families.

OVERLAPPING SPACES

For the majority of our respondents, who do not work full-time, the "sensed environment" is for the most part limited to the home; therefore the overlap between fantasy and household is perhaps a more precise measure of the degree to which fantasy reflects the sensed environment than are the data used in the last chapter.

Our analysis is, again, based on the "think about" question. The question now is: How many of the people thought about live with the respondent?

The relevant data are presented in Table 4-1. The first column in this table shows the percentage of people thought about who also live in the household. The table divides nonhousehold fantasy figures into children (column 2) and others (column 3).

There is a general decline in overlap as people are older, until we get to those over seventy-four, for whom the figure is 7 percent. It would be quite understandable for our old people to feel lonely, since just about none of the people they think about lived with them. For young people there is fairly high overlap with about half the people thought about living with the respondent.

Comparing whites and blacks of the same age, there is a general tendency for blacks to have less overlap. This would be consistent with the data in the last chapter, which suggested that blacks give more significance to the extended family. As a result there is somewhat less congruence for black women between their fantasy and their daily sensed environment.

If we compare Tables 3-11 and 4-1 we see that in the latter table the degree of overlap between fantasy and the environment is more consistently related to age. Table 3-11 refers to the degree to which fantasy figures are not part of the sensed environment for long periods of time, while Table 4-1 refers more

TABLE 4–1

PERCENT OF FANTASY COEXTENSIVE WITH HOUSEHOLD AND NUCLEAR FAMILY: BY COLOR AND AGE OF RESPONDENT

(Percentages based on number of actual responses)

Color & Age	Percent of fantasy figures living in respondents households	Percent of fantasy figures who are respondents children not living in respondents households	Percent of fantasy figures not included in previous two columns	Subsample size
White 17–19	—%	—%	—%	(9)[1]
20–29	46	0	54	(26)
30–39	34	1	65	(65)
40–49	37	18	45	(67)
50–59	28	26	46	(81)
60–74	14	23	63	(112)
75 plus	7	34	59	(41)
Black 17–19	42	0	58	(31)
20–29	34	2	64	(338)
30–39	32	5	63	(273)
40–49	30	10	60	(168)
50–59	19	11	70	(80)
60–74	7	24	69	(100)
75 plus	—	—	—	(6)

1. In parentheses is the number of persons named in response to the "think about" question.

TABLE 4–2

PERCENT OF FANTASY FIGURES WHO LIVE WITH RESPONDENT OR
ARE RESPONDENTS' OWN CHILDREN LIVING AWAY FROM HOME

(By age and color of respondent.)

	Color	
Age	White	Black
17–19	—[1]	42
20–29	46	36
30–39	35	37
40–49	55	40
50–59	54	30
60–74	37	31
75 plus	41	—[2]

1. There were only nine respondents in this category, which seemed too few to analyze.

2. There were only six respondents in this category.

to the respondents' daily experience. Is a sense of alienation more closely related to daily experience or to longer time periods? Would the results in Table 3-11 or those in Table 4-1 be more closely related to a sense of alienation? At present all we can do is point to the problem of determining what are the subjectively meaningful time intervals in people's lives.

As a minimum it is assumed that the respondent is more likely to experience some alienation if the fantasy does not mirror the environment at the time of the fantasy. Therefore, Table 4-1 would seem to present the better data, for it can safely be assumed that much of the respondents' fantasizing will take place in the home, and therefore if the fantasy objects do not live with the respondent, it would be highly unlikely that fantasy would mirror the sensed environment. But, does this objective alienation produce different amounts of subjective alienation depending on whether the respondent is going to see the nonhouseholder thought about in the next few days or weeks? It seems possible. That is, if a woman daydreams about a son who lives around the corner and whom she will see tomorrow, this would have a different effect than if she daydreamed about a dead son. It may be worthwhile to do research on the problem of whether the alienating effect of non-overlapping environments is affected by the anticipation of contact with the person thought about; if such anticipation is significant, the effects of different time intervals between the fantasy and the anticipated contact with the fantasized object should then be explored.

One obvious explanation for the decline in the overlap of fantasy and household as people become older would be the maturing of children with the result that they leave the home—at least in the United States. This would mean that columns 1 and 2 in Table 4-1, when added together, should show no change with age, i.e., if we add together involvement with household members and involvement in nonhousehold children the resulting percentages should be the same for all ages. Table 4-2 shows this combined total in relation to age and color. For whites, there is a curvilinear relationship. In the younger and older years the percentages are about the same, while between the ages of forty and fifty-nine the percentage is unusally high. For the whites, then, it can not be said that the low percentages for the older respondents are due simply to their children moving out; this cannot explain the difference in Table 4-2 between those forty to fifty-nine and those sixty and over.

For blacks there is not the curvilinear relation found for whites,[1] but there is a decline in percentages as people get older, although the decline begins earlier for blacks than for whites.

In short, as Table 4-2 shows there is still a difference by age even when

TABLE 4–3

PERCENT OF DIFFERENT CATEGORIES OF PEOPLE (OTHER THAN CHILDREN) PRESENT IN RESPONDENTS' HOUSEHOLDS WHO ARE THOUGHT ABOUT

Relation	Number thought about	Number in households	Percent thought about[1]
Roomer[2]	2	42	5
Friend[2]	1	12	8
Grandparent (or parent)[3]	6	21	29
Sibling	4	37	11
Spouse[4]	155	370	42
Other relative	4	59	7
Children at home, but not respondents' own	1	87	1

1. This percent overestimates the number thought about, since the number thought about is based on N=623, while the number in a household is based on N=608. It seemed unnecessary to refine our analysis to justify the basic conclusions stated in the text. Two adults are not included because of improper coding.

2. These categories were used by the respondent.

3. This category refers to the homemaker's parents.

4. In some cases the homemakers's parents are included. This happened because the code used was "spouse or parent," and when no grandchildren were present in the home, the homemaker's parents were coded with the same number as spouses. So, there were eight married women who were coded as having two spouses; in fact, of course, this meant simply that the homemaker's mother or father was living in the home, but there were no grandchildren at home. Such miscoded grandparents could not be separated in the analysis from spouses. But there were few such cases.

TABLE 4–4

PERCENT OF DIFFERENT AGE AGGREGATES OF RESPONDENTS'
OWN CHILDREN WHO ARE THOUGHT ABOUT[1]

Age of children	Number thought about	Number respondents have	Percent thought about
0–4	71	236	30
5–6	25	167	15
7–13	69	508	14
14–16	23	138	17
17 and above			
at home	56	138	41
other	114	310	37

1. Our respondents thought about 6 dead children; these are not included in the table.

we combine columns 1 and 2 in Table 4-1. The decline in overlap of fantasy and household that occurs for older people can not be explained simply by the fact that mature children leave home.

Another explanation for the absence of overlap is that people live alone. But this assumes that if people do live together they will fantasize abouut each other, and as will be seen in the next section this is not always true.

The main point of this section is that in our sample there is a basis for considerable alienation, since for no age-range does the overlap of fantasy and household reach 50 percent. Moreover, this overlap declines as age increases, reaching an amazingly low 7 percent for the elderly.

FAMILY INVOLVEMENT

In this section we shall analyze the nature of family involvement, still making use of the "think about" question. We assume that the objects in fantasy are the ones with whom the respondent is most involved, i.e., we use the "think about" question as a crude measure of involvement.

In Chapter One it was suggested that spatial closeness itself produces involvement. In a related discussion Adams has suggested that the effect of physical distance varies directly with biological distance, i.e., as biological distance decreases, the effects of physical distance decline. Adam's point is that biological distance is much more important than physical distance.[2] This would mean, for instance, that our respondents should be less involved with distant relatives living in the household than with close relatives living outside the household. Is this true?

Table 4-3 shows the percent of different categories of people living with the respondent who are thought about. Table 4-4 shows the percent of the respondents' own (i.e., by birth, not marriage or adoption) children who are thought about.

If the percentage for children seventeen years of age and over who are not living at home is compared with the other figure in Tables 4-3 and 4-4 we can see the relative importance of physical and of biological distance. First, note that the percentage for these children is just about the same as for children of the same age who are living at home. The fact of co-residence with the respondent seems inconsequential. Second, if we compare adult children living away from home with other categories of relatives living with the respondent, and leaving aside for a moment the case of spouses, it is clear that involvement seems more affected by the biological closeness of children than by the physical closeness of roomers, friends, siblings, and other relatives. But the relative importance of biological and physical distance is no better illustrated than by comparing adult children not living in their parent's home (37 percent of whom are thought about) and children not the respondent's own but living with the respondent (1 percent of whom are thought about). The latter category is quite mixed, including stepchildren, grandchildren, children of a sibling and the like, but the very low percentage for this category suggests that all these types of relation amount to the same thing for the respondent. In a related study, Bowerman and Irish found that stepchildren felt less affection than natural children for their parents.[3] It is quite clear that biological distance minimizes, if not eliminates, the effects of physical distance.

A closer examination of Tables 4-3 and 4-4, however, calls into question even the significance of biological distance. First, the highest percentage (42 percent) is for spouses, with whom the respondents have no biological relationship. Second, the respondents have an equal biological relation with their own parents and with their children, but the latter are more frequently listed by the respondents as fantasy objects; equal biological distance does not mean equal chances of being fantasy objects. Third, there is little significant difference between non-relatives living with the respondent such as roomers (5 percent) and friends (8 percent) and certain kind of relatives also living with the respondent such as siblings (11 percent) and "other relatives" (7 percent). As already discussed, it is assumed that fantasizing about an object is a sign of involvement with that object. Given this assumption, the results just noted indicate that social involvement does not seem simply to reflect biological distance.

The data in Tables 4-3 and 4-4, then, do not support the idea that either physical or biological distance is important to involvement. What is important is the nuclear family. Outside this unit involvement is scattered among different types of people, although parents do stand out from other categories of people. This scattering of involvement outside the nuclear family, however,

TABLE 4-5

PERCENT OF MARRIED RESPONDENTS WHO THINK ABOUT
THEIR SPOUSE

(By age and color of respondent[1])

Age	White		Black	
	%	N	%	N
17–19	—	(2)	—	(9)
20–29	—	(7)	42	(83)
30–39	47	(15)	48	(75)
40–49	45	(20)	63	(32)
50–59	39	(26)	60	(10)
60–74	27	(22)	17	(12)
75 plus	—	(4)	—	(1)

1. Actually the percentages refer to the number of people coded "5" who are thought about. Code "5" refers to either spouse or parent, but for our married respondents there are only a few cases in which "5" refers to parents. Eliminating such cases would have been time-consuming and would not have changed the pattern of results.

might be affected by physical distance, i.e., the friends or sisters or aunts we become involved with might be those who are physically close to us; our research could neither confirm nor deny this.

There appears to be a curvilinear relation between the age of children and the percent who are thought about (see Table 4-4). Among nonadult children only the very young have a good chance to be thought about. This could be

TABLE 4-6

PERCENT OF MARRIED RESPONDENTS WHO THINK ABOUT
THEIR SPOUSE

(By color and age of respondents and number of cities and towns lived in by respondents[1])

Number of cities and towns lived in	Age and color					
	17–29		30–39		40–59	
	White	Black	White	Black	White	Black
	% N	% N	% N	% N	% N	% N
1–2	— (7)	42 (57)	— (8)	44 (41)	33 (36)	42 (26)
3 or more	— (2)	39 (41)	— (8)	53 (31)	60 (10)	70 (20)

1. There are too few cases aged 60 and above to analyze.

due to differences in family size, i.e., only the very young children in our sample are likely to be the only child in their family; all of the older children are likely to have at least one sibling at home. But it is also true that very young children do demand more attention from their parents than older children. We are assuming of course, that the frequency with which children of a certain age are thought about is a crude measure of the average degree of parental involvement with children at that age; thus, since children between five and six are less frequently thought about than children four or younger, we assume that mothers generally are more involved with the younger children. The curvilinear relation suggested by Table 4-4 between age and involvement will be made use of later on in the chapter when we discuss the natural history of familial involvement.

Although the data in Table 4-3 point to the importance of the spouse, it cannot be ignored that only 42 percent of the spouses living with our respondents were mentioned in response to the "think about" question. We attempted to explore the nature of the husband-wife relationship further. Table 4-5 shows the percent of respondents who think about the spouse by age and color of respondent. For the whites there is an inverse relation between the percentage and age; when the white women are older, fewer of them think about their spouse. For blacks, there seems to be a curvilinear relation between the percentage and age. A very high percentage of black women between ages forty and fifty-nine think about their spouse. In general, black women seem more involved with their husbands than do the white women. However, among both whites and blacks, husband-wife involvement seems less frequent among the elderly than among the rest of the sample.

The expected pattern of involvement among spouses would be similar to that found by Blood and Wolfe in their study of Detroit families. They reported the wife's mean marital satisfaction by stages in the family life cycles as follows:

Honeymoon	4.26
Preschool	3.99
Preadolescent	3.91
Adolescent Children	3.76
Post-Adolescent Children at Home	3.50
Postparental	3.83
Retired	3.80[4]

This pattern shows an end-of-the-cycle upsurge not found in our data. This may reflect sample differences. On the other hand, a satisfaction index, which was the measure used by Blood and Wolfe, is difficult to interpret, because it reflects both the amount of involvement and the expectations about involvement. A person may be satisfied either because she is highly involved or because she is not involved with her husband very much but does not desire high involvement. A measure of satisfaction can not be used as a measure of involvement. In spite of Blood and Wolfe's work, therefore, it is possible that spousal alienation in old age, as suggested by our data, does occur.

Why might there be a turning away from the spouse in old age? We suggest this happens because the types of problems that occur as people become old are unrelated to the reasons for the choice of a spouse. For many old people, interest in sex declines. Interest in dancing, going to parties, and perhaps even a general interest in fun, diminishes. Children have left the home, so the fatherly characteristics of a husband which might have been important at the time of marriage are in old age less significant. Elderly people face new problems centering on illness, loneliness, and retirement. The strengths of a man that make him a desirable husband may not be relevant to helping wives solve the new problems of old age. As a result elderly women may have to look elsewhere—to children or to members of the extended family or to God or to themselves—for the resources needed to survive in the last stage of the life-cycle.

But even if this is true, we have hardly begun to explain why less than half of the married respondents mentioned their husband in response to the "think about" question. One possible source of light is Elizabeth Bott's discussion of mobility and family ties.

> Networks [of relationships] become dispersed when people move around from one place to another...their [i.e., spouses] external relationships are relatively discontinuous both in space and in time. Such continuity as they possess lies in their relationship with each other rather than in their external relationships. In facing the external world, they draw on each other, for their strongest emotional investment is made where there is continuity.

Mobility makes nonhousehold relationships discontinuous, but "emotional investment" follows continuous lines therefore mobile people are more involved with their spouses. Key concepts such as "continuity" and "emotional investment" are not clearly defined, but the basic prediction relating mobility and the marital bond is clear. Table 4-6 shows the relation between spousal involvement and the number of different towns and cities the respondent has lived in; the latter seemed to be the measure of mobility that best expressed Bott's idea of continuity. It can be assumed that the continuity of relations with nonhousehold members would be seriously affected by a move from one town to another. In general the data in Table 4-6 support Bott's hypothesis. Clearly, among the respondents thirty to fifty-nine years of age those who have lived in three or more places seem more involved in their spouses. The lack of significant results for those seventeen to twenty-nine does not necessarily contradict Bott; the question used in the interview did not allow us to categorize respondents on the basis of the number of places lived since marriage, but since birth; this failure would be especially crucial for the younger respondents, more of whose moves probably occurred before marriage. It is best, therefore, not to consider the young respondents. In general, then, our data support Bott's idea that involvement is related to continuity.

The problem we are discussing is why only 42 percent of the spouses are thought about by our respondents, It has been suggested that this might be due: 1) to the fact that the characteristics relevant to mate selection may be irrelevant to being able to adjust in old age, and that therefore aging wives may have to seek help from people other than the spouse who have the needed resources, and 2) if families are not mobile, then continuity is not limited to the marriage relationship. Our comments perhaps shed some light on the problem, but it is still far from clear why so many spouses are not frequently thought about. It is possible that the "think about" question, contrary to what we hoped, measured only positive involvement. Wives might have mentioned their spouses only if they were happily married. Even though people may think about people they dislike, they may suppress the memories of such fantasies. It remains a question whether the problem is why so many wives dislike their spouses or why so many are relatively uninvolved with their spouses. In either case, more research is needed that attempts to measure the involvement, as defined in Chapter One, of husband and wives with each other. Why are so few spouses mentioned in response to the "think about" question?

THE QUALITY OF INVOLVEMENT

In the last section we discussed the distribution of involvement—whether respondents are involved with people they live with, and whether they are involved with their children and their husband. The question was simply whether or not involvement existed. Now we shall begin a consideration of the quality of this involvement. In what ways are our respondents involved with their family?

COMMUNICATION

About each person a respondent thought about we asked: "Do you discuss your really personal problems with (person mentioned)?" We used this question as an indicator of the extent to which involvement is based on knowledge.

There are some problems in using the discussion question as a measure of knowledge. Besides the fact that some people will lie, a positive answer does not always mean the same thing, i.e., a person might reveal much more of herself in some discussions than in others. Moreover, this question examines a relationship from only one side; it tells us nothing about how much the other person reveals to our respondent. Finally, inter-personal knowledge is not totally dependent on self-revelation; some people will know us better than others simply because they have lived with us, and had more occasions to observe us. Still, it seems clear that a positive response to the discussion question indicates that interpersonal knowledge exists in a relationship.

Table 4-7 shows the frequency respondents discuss their personal problems with different categories of people. The distinctiveness of the marital relationship in American society is clearly indicated by the extremely high percentage of respondents who discuss their personal problems with their husbands; of course, we must remember that only half of the existing spouses are thought about. As we would expect, revelation to children increases as the children age; the fact that any revelation occurs with children under seven is surprising, and might simply indicate the looseness with which some people interpreted the question. The data do indicate the problem of children; they are objects of maternal involvement, but until they become teenagers no signifi-

TABLE 4–7

PERCENT OF TYPES OF PEOPLE WHO ARE THOUGHT ABOUT WITH WHOM RESPONDENTS DISCUSS THEIR PERSONAL PROBLEMS[1]

Type of person thought about		Percent with whom discuss personal problems	
		%	N
Spouses		91	(147)
Others living with respondents (excluding own children)		61	(13)
Others not living with respondents (excluding children)		55	(718)
Children:	0–4 years old:		
	at home	9	(56)
	other	—	(9)
	5–6 years old:		
	at home	35	(26)
	other	—	(1)
	7–13 years old:		
	at home	42	(60)
	other	—	(3)
	14–16 years old:		
	at home	57	(21)
	other	—	(2)
	17 and over:		
	at home	69	(48)
	other	64	(104)

1. We excluded persons thought about for whom there was a "no response" on the discussion question or the question asking respondents to list the members of their household. In this table we are referring only to respondents coded as either white or black.

cant personal communication takes place with most of them. Women can be involved with their environment and yet feel lonely, because often they are involved with children who are incapable of understanding them. For those women who believe that being understood as a person is a major part of personal relationships,involvement with children can be a cause of loneliness.

On the other hand more self-revelation takes place with adult children than with other adults, excluding spouses of course. However, the differences are small. Respondents discuss their problems with 69 percent of the adult children at home and with 61 percent of all others at home who are thought about; the difference of 8 percent is small. The difference between adult children not at home and other adults not living with the respondent is only 9 percent. Among people significant enough to be thought about, self-revelation does not seem more likely to children than to other types of acquaintances. Personal communication distinguishes only the husband-wife relation.

It is quite clear from Table 4-7 that the quality of the parent-child relation changes as the child ages. The older the child the more likely he or she is to be a confidant for our respondents.

It might be asked how meaningful can the discussion question be when 35 percent of the children five to six years of age are supposedly confidants for their mothers. It is possible that our respondents answered the question too hastily. But there are several other explanations. Perhaps, when children are young, mothers tell them their problems, but without expecting any answers; talking to young children who cannot help may be better than talking to four walls. It is also possible that mothers may discuss their problems in only a superficial way with young children. Again, it is possible that in some cases the mother's problems involve the children, making some mothers treat children like adults. In a study of lower-class families, Pavenstedt found that in thirty stable families parents did not seem to distinguish between children and adults—"they projected adult comprehension and responses onto the infants, sometimes even the newborn."[6] Future studies of communication should not overlook the possibility that in daily life some people may not distinguish between children and adults.

Despite the fact that children are communicated with even at a young age, the fact should not be lost sight of that one-third of the adult children thought about are not confidants for the mothers. Children, on the whole, never seem to reach the level of confidence experienced by husbands.

The very high percentage of thought-about husbands with whom respondents discuss their problems raises the issue whether the "think about" question is measuring only positive involvement. Theoretically, people who are loved or hated should be thought about. But only a loved person is likely to be a confidant. The high percentage of spouses with whom the respondents communicate could be explained, then, in two ways: 1) The "think about"

TABLE 4–8

PERCENT OF PEOPLE THOUGHT ABOUT WITH WHOM RESPONDENT
DISCUSSES PERSONAL PROBLEMS

(By age and color of respondent.[1])

Age	Color			
	White		Black	
	%	N	%	N
17–19	—	(9)	57	(30)
20–29	50	(22)	47	(303)
30–39	60	&85')	57	(245)
40–49	61	(52)	64	(143)
50–59	61	(72)	67	(72)
60–74	63	(92)	54	(83)
75 and over	52	(20)	—	(5)

1. Totals on which percentages are based do not include cases in which the respondents did not answer the question about with whom they discuss their personal problems.

question reflects only positive involvement; 2) Our respondents do not continue to live with spouses they hate, so they are likely to feel either love or indifference or something in between toward their husbands, but not hate. Our data do not allow us to choose between these explanations. It is possible, therefore, that the "think about" question is biased and indicates only positive involvement.

Komarovsky has discussed the network of confidants that existed in her lower-class sample. "Two-thirds of the wives had at least one person apart from their husbands in whom they confide deeply personal experiences. In 35 percent of the cases the wife...shares some significant segment of her life *more fully* with her confidants than with her husband."[7] The evidence from our study certainly does not contradict this description. In Table 4-1 it can be seen what percent of the fantasy refers to people who are not members of the nuclear family (column 3); in fact, this percentage is an underestimation, since it does not include the nonnuclear-family people living with the respondent who are thought about. Except for middle-aged whites, it is over 45 percent. In other words, it is certainly true that our respondents are involved with many individuals who come from outside their nuclear families. If, now, we look at Table 4-7 it can be seen that respondents discuss their personal problems with 55 percent of those people who do not live with the respondents and who are not the respondents's children. Our data, therefore, support Komarovksy's point that lower class women are involved in a network of relationships outside the nuclear family in which they discuss their personal experiences.

TABLE 4–9

PERCENT OF CERTAIN TYPES OF PEOPLE WHOM RESPONDENTS
THINK ABOUT, AND WITH WHOM THEY DISCUSS
PERSONAL PROBLEMS

(By age and color of respondent)

Type of people	Age and color					
	40–59		60–74		75 and over	
	White	Black	White	Black	White	Black
	% N	% N	% N	% N	% N	% N
Spouse	94 (17)	88 (25)	— (5)	— (2)	— (2)	— (1)
Adult children at home	87 (15)	56 (16)	— (2)	— (2)	— (0)	— (0)
Away	48 (23)	67 (18)	86 (21)	60 (20)	67 (12)	— (2)
Other adults not living with respondents	54 (52)	64 (131)	46 (56)	50 (54)	29 (54)	— (1)

What is the quality of our respondents' pattern of involvement? Table 4-8 shows the percent of all the people thought about with whom the respondents discuss their personal problems. Overall there is a curvilinear relation with age; young and old communicate with fewer people with whom they are involved than do the middle-aged. For the young respondents the low percentage no doubt reflects the difficulty of communicating with children. Among women fifty years of age and over the main categories of confidants are spouses, adult children, and other nonhousehold adults. Table 4-9 shows the percent of people in each of these categories with whom respondents discuss their personal problems. The numbers in the cells of the table are small; moreover, it must be remembered that the cell frequencies refer not to respondents but confidants so that the number of respondents referred to in each cell is no doubt smaller than the number shown. The data can only be viewed as suggestive, but they do seem to help us in understanding the meaning of Table 4-8. As can be seen in Table 4-9 spouses become insignificant for respondents sixty and over; in part this is due to the death of spouses and in part to the apparently low involvement among old spouses in our sample. The significance of this loss is magnified among black women, because it accompanies a general decline in self-revelation; older black women in our sample seem to communicate less often with both adult children and nonhousehold adults. On the other hand, white women seem to compensate for the loss of spouse by dramatically increasing the frequency with which they communicate with their adult chil-

SOLIDARITY IN A SLUM

dren who live away from home; the frequency increases from 48 percent to 86 percent. In part, then, the lower frequency of self-revelation among black women in the sixty to seventy-four age range seems due to their failure to increase communication with their adult children as they enter old age.

The low frequency of communication among the white women seventy-four and over is due to a general decline in self-revelation. It can not be forgotten that the truly elderly women who are left in a place like Kilbourntown might never in their lives have experienced much communication. Our study has not been able to follow the same people over time; therefore we cannot conclude that the respondents, who are now sixty to seventy-four years old, when they are over seventy-four will show a decline in self-revelation. The type of person who is seventy-five or more and lives in Kilbourntown might be quite different from the type of person who is a resident of K-3 and in the sixty to seventy-four age range. But one of our purposes in this chapter is to develop a tentative model for a "natural history of familial involvement." To accomplish this we are acting *as if* we had studied the same people throughout their lives.

It is important to note that in at least one-third of the cases the people thought about are not confidants. There is ample basis for feelings of loneliness in Kilbourntown, if we define loneliness as a sense of not being known as we perceive ourselves. Our homemakers are involved in many relationships in which they do not reveal what is most important to them. Such impersonal involvements would seem highly likely to produce a sense of loneliness. It is possible that the effect of noncommunication varies depending on the social object, i.e., depending on whether a person is involved with God, a deceased relative, a young child, and so on. But the refinement of an understanding concerning the cause of loneliness suggested by this line of reasoning we leave to another time.

Moreover, our data no doubt overestimate how much communication does take place. The general point that husbands and wives in the United States do communicate is supported by the work of Blood and Wolfe. They report in their study of Detroit house-wives that 40 percent of the wives said their husbands tell them about events at work daily, 37 percent said it happened at least once a week, and only 7 percent said their husbands never tell them about their work.[8] But both our study and the Detroit study have at least two major weaknesses: 1) there was no measure of actual information transferred, and 2) there was no control on the significance of the specific events discussed. A study that did seek specific information was reported by Babchuk and Bates. They asked thirty-nine couples to name close, mutual friends. Of the 277 friends mentioned, 118 were listed by both spouses. Over half of the supposed "mutual friends" were not mentioned by both spouses.[9] No doubt other studies of husband-wife communication on specific topics would, also, reveal considerable ignorance of each other's thoughts.

Because of its vagueness and perhaps because some of our respondents thought they "should" be discussing their problems with their close relatives and friends, and therefore gave the socially right but not the true answer, the discussion question probably overestimates the amount of self-revelation that takes place. Given this fact, why did our question reveal as much noncommunication as it did? First, there is the obvious problem with children: until they mature, meaningful communication is not possible. Second, it seems likely that some people restrict self-revelation in order to differentiate the spousal relationship. In her study of working-class families, Komarovsky reported the following:

> The young woman made a deliberate effort, after her engagement, to become more reserved with her mother. "I wanted," she explained, "to feel closer to John than to Mother, so that when we are all together I would exchange a look of understanding with him and not with her."[10]

This woman regulated her flow of communication to develop a desired pattern of involvement; no doubt there are norms, however vague, that outline some rank-order of involvement, and these are reflected in the pattern of communication. Third, the pattern of communication is probably related to liking as suggested by Jourard;[11] communication, then, would be greatest in the spousal relation, because of all family relations it is the most freely chosen; it is the most voluntary relation, and therefore the one most based on liking as opposed to role-obligation. Giving information is a way of solidifying a relationship, so we would be more likely to reveal ourselves in relationships that are more intrinsically satisfying, i.e., we tend to communicate freely to the extent an object is a direct source of reward and therefore liked. The distribution of self-revelation, therefore, is likely to reflect both relevant norms about communication and the liking pattern. For our respondents the result of probably these and other processes is that between one-third and one half, depending on age, of their involvement is impersonal.

POWER

By power is meant the extent to which one person determines the life of another. No one has succeeded yet in devising an adequate measure of this concept. In our case we used two questions: "Which person do you most often go to for advice when you have money problems?" And: "Which person do you most often go to for advice when you have family problems?" The responses used by the interviewer were: "solves own problem," "goes to no *one* person," and "goes to someone." If the interviewee went to someone, we asked about the respondent's relation to her advisor.

There are some obvious problems with our measure of power. First, it is assumed that the advisors' comments will actually affect our respondents' behavior. Second, even if the question does reflect power, it fails to indicate, except crudely, the amount of power. If someone's advice about money problems is followed, to what extent does that determine our respondents' behavior? We cannot tell. Third, the questions refer only to extraordinary circumstances; they do not tell us who is shaping the everyday life of our respondents. Although true, this last criticism is not as significant as might first appear, because: (a) controlling what a person does at moments of crisis affects the total pattern of a person's life; day-to-day influences only modify this pattern; so, giving advice on whether a mother should work can result in a totally new family arrangement, which daily decisions would only modify, and b) a person's *sense* of dependence on another is probably determined more by what happens at these moments of heightened self-consciousness than by daily, often little-noticed events. We think, therefore, that from the point-of-view of both objective and subjective involvement, it is meaningful to measure power by asking about the people our respondents go to when they have significant problems.

We restricted our questions to the two types of problems most likely to be universal in a low-income area. It should be noted that our questions do not prejudge who might be significant in a person's life. One of the weaknesses of some measures of family power is that the questions assume that power resides either with the husband or the wife, i,e., within the nuclear family; we make no assumptions about the distribution of power. (It is true that the questions are worded to force the respondent to name someone; this was done because we feared that a more permissive question would have resulted in everyone saying they go to no one; however, our alternative responses did allow for such an answer, so that the interviewers did not feel compelled to force the respondent to name someone.) It is important to remember that everyone in the course of life faces family and money problems. These problems have arisen in our respondents' lives, and someone has determined their reactions. Who?

Table 4-10 shows the percentage of respondents who seek advice for either money or family problems. Regarding money matters there is some difference between whites and blacks in the middle years, with the blacks seeking advice more often. Concerning family problems the most striking fact is the small percentage (5 percent) of black women sixty to seventy-four who seek advice on family matters; among the whites there is a slight decrease among the older people. The most important point, however, is that the overwhelming majority of our respondents said they solve their own problems.

In their survey of Detroit housewives Blood and Wolfe asked: "Every wife has some days when things go so badly that she gets pretty tense and upset. After you've had a bad day, what do you do to get it out of your system?" Only 33 percent mentioned some form of interaction with others. The authors conclude: "Clearly, most housewives cope with bad days on their own. Their most characteristic device is to go to bed early, to sit down and relax, or just try to forget about their troubles. Reading and television are common distractions at home, with going for a walk the favorite way of getting out of the house."[12]

Similarly, in a study done in Cleveland with both working-and middle-class families, Sussman found that only 31 percent of the respondents reported giving or receiving advice on personal or business matters; this study gathered data only on the respondents's relation to kin, but, as our study suggests, this is probably the major source of advice.[13] When we combined responses to our two advice questions, we found that about 30 percent have sought advice from someone on at least one problem. The rough similarity of percentages from Blood and Wolfe, Sussman, and our research suggests that our results are valid.

It is usual in family research to assume that inter-personal power exists between spouses, and that what is not known is the distribution of this power between husband and wife. For instance, a researcher might select a list of topics related to family behaviour, e.g., whether to buy a home or should children work, and ask who decides these questions. Power is measured by the frequency a spouse makes a decision. There are certain obvious difficulties with

TABLE 4–10

PERCENT WHO SEEK ADVICE FROM ANOTHER PERSON ON MONEY
AND ON FAMILY PROBLEMS

	(By age and color of respondent)							
	Money problems				Family problems			
Age	White		Black		White		Black	
	%	N	%	N	%	N	%	N
17–19	—	(3)	76	(11)	—	(3)	36	(11)
20–29	27	(11)	26	(133)	18	(11)	24	(133)
30–39	16	(25)	24	(110)	16	(25)	26	(111)
40–49	15	(26)	22	(69)	23	(26)	17	(69)
50–59	24	(33)	33	(34)	13	(32)	21	(34)
60–74	23	(47)	24	(38)	15	(48)	5	(38)
75 plus	10	(20)	—	(2)	10	(20)	—	(2)
No response	—	(3)	—	(8)	—	(3)	—	(8)
		(168[1])		(405[2])		(168[1])		(405[2])

1. One white respondent said she talked with several different people.

2. Four black respondents said they talked with several other people or gave no response.

SOLIDARITY IN A SLUM

this approach which need not be discussed here (e.g., how to select the topics). What our results, and to some extent the results of the Detroit study, suggest is that many problems faced by adults never reach any stage requiring a dyadic or group decision. Much more than research seems to allow, people try to solve their own problems; they do not allow the matter to develop to the point that a joint decision is required. Too much sociological research assumes a complete social distribution of power; our results suggest the opposite; more than we realize, people determine their own lives.

Such statements as were just made may be called sociologically naive. It is true that to talk about a person determining his own life is to oversimplify. What we want to emphasize is that apparently a significant number of problems are solved or ameliorated without individuals believing that they had been directly dependent on the intentional acts of others.

Power requires that we be determined by acts of others, which acts, in turn, are controlled by these other people. Apparently many people do not experience this type of event, contrary to what sociologists are prone to assume. It might be argued that our respondents simply misrepresented their situations; people do not like to admit dependence, so they "forget" it. Or, perhaps people do not often seek advice, but they are in fact constantly receiving it, but in little doses, so that it goes unrecognized. No doubt people do "forget," and no doubt advice oozes through the social structures. We still contend, however, that given the overwhelming majority of respondents who said they solve their own problems, sociologists must spend more time determining the extent to which interpersonal power exists, before exploring the form of distribution for whatever social power does exist.

To whom do the respondents go for advice other than themselves? Table 4-11 presents the relevant data. Regardless of type of problem or color of respondent, a majority of advice comes from outside the nuclear family. Perhaps because the two types of problems often involve members of the immediate family, their advice is not sought. This would help us understand why so many of the respondents solve their own problems. For instance, their problems might often involve their spouse in such a way as to prevent his being used as a source of advice. In some cases, in fact, the problem might be the spouse. But since he is the person with whom our respondents are most likely to be open with, the husband's involvement in the problem might result in the wives feeling a sense of "nowhere to turn." From this perspective, the respondents' independence is the result of the absence of suitable sources of advice.

Overall, about 25 percent of the advice comes from an impersonal source, such as a welfare worker, a lawyer, or a doctor, while the greatest source is clearly the extended family: siblings, parents, and other relatives. At least one-third of the advice on a problem comes from this category, and for family problems over half of the advice sought by black respondents was from the

TABLE 4–11

RELATION OF PEOPLE RESPONDENTS SEEK ADVICE FROM ON MONEY AND ON FAMILY PROBLEMS

(By color of respondent)

Relation	Money problems		Family problems	
	White(N=35)	Black(N=101)	White(N=27)	Black(N=85)
Spouse (or other adult in residence)[1]	31%	19%	11%	1%
Children	9	7	11	3
Siblings	14	14	4	14
Parents not living with the respondents	11	14	7	26
Other relatives	9	5	22	17
Friends	6	8	19	15
Impersonal sources	20	33	26	24

1. Our coding does not allow us to differentiate spouses from other adults in residence with respondent (children excluded); we assume most of those mentioned are spouses.

extended family. The immediate family of spouse and children is a significant source of advice only among whites in matters of money, in which case 40 percent of the advice is from the nuclear family. Table 4-12 shows the same data as Table 4-11 except that the former is limited to cases in which the

TABLE 4–12

RELATION OF PEOPLE RESPONDENTS SEEK ADVICE FROM ON MONEY AND ON FAMILY PROBLEMS BY COLOR OF RESPONDENT

(For married respondents only)

Relation	Money problems		Family problems	
	White(N=20)	Black(N=56)	White(N=12)	Black(N=41)
Spouse (or other adult in residence)	55%	31%	25%	2%
Children	5	6	8	0
Siblings	10	10	0	7
Parents not living with re- spondents	5	12	8	20
Other relatives	10	7	25	24
Friends	0	4	8	22
Impersonal sources	15	30	25	24

respondent is married. The overall pattern in the two tables is the same. White women make more use of their husbands than do black women. In fact, regarding family problems almost 5 percent of the black married respondents seek advice outside even the extended family: they go to friends or impersonal sources. Although the husband-wife relation among blacks and whites does not significantly differ regarding communication, there appears to be a difference on power; black wives less often seek advice from their spouses.

If we compare money and family problems, the latter more often force respondents outside even the extended family. Almost half the help sought on family problems comes from friends and impersonal sources. There seems to be a process at work that makes involvement self-limiting. What we mean is this: As people become involved with others, say the family, more and more problems will be related to the family; but since apparently people seek advice outside the institutional source of problems, as family problems increase involvement in some other institutional area will increase. It appears as if individuals try to segregate the source of a problem from the advisor on a problem. As a result, involvement in any one institution or group will tend to be self-limiting.

For our respondents the result is a scattering of involvement outside the family.

The fact that even for whites the nuclear family does not dominate the advice pattern is consistent with Gans's comment on spouses living in a lower-class Boston district: "They take their troubles less to each other than to brothers, sisters, other relatives, or friends."[14] Similarly Komarovsky, based on an intensive study of sixty lower-class families, concluded that "these men and women do not turn to one another for emotional support. ..."[15] Not only do our respondents tend to solve their own problems, but they also tend, with the exception of white women who have money problems, to go outside the nuclear family when they do seek advice.

Table 4-13 shows the rank order for the various sources of advice. Clearly the professional sources stand out over any one familial category; only the spouse approximates the significance of professional people in guiding our slum respondents. This fact underlines the necessity, especially in lower-class families, of not assuming that significant decisions are made within the family.

The rank order on money problems is very similar for whites and blacks, but the two aggregates differ somewhat on how they solve family problems. As already noted, the spouse has an insignificant role to play for the black women who have family problems; on the other hand their parents are dramatically more important for them than for whites. A word of warning is, however, needed; this difference in the importance of parents reflects, at least in part, the different age structures for whites and blacks. The relatively small number of people who seek help made a detailed color-age analysis useless, but

TABLE 4–13

RANK ORDER OF TYPES OF PEOPLE RESPONDENTS SEEK ADVICE
FROM ON MONEY AND ON FAMILY PROBLEMS

(By color of respondent)

Relation	Money problems		Family problems	
	White	Black	White	Black
Spouse (or adult in residence)	1	2	4	7
Children	5	6	4	6
Siblings	3	3	7	5
Parents not living with respondents	4	3	6	1
Other relatives	5	7	2	3
Friends	7	5	3	4
Impersonal sources	2			2

we must not forget that the white population is much older. This no doubt accounts at least for some of the difference between whites and blacks regarding parental significance. On the other hand the similarity of rank order for the two color-aggregates on money problems suggests that age differences are not the whole explanation for differences regarding family problems. Moreover the greater significance of parents for black women fits the general finding that the black respondents are more involved with their extended family. It should be remembered, however, that this difference does not exist for money problems; greater black dependence on extended kin occurs only for the more personal family problems.

The slightly greater significance of "children" for the whites is probably explainable in terms of the greater age of the white children. It is interesting that siblings decline in relative importance as we shift from money to family problems; on the other hand, "other relatives" and friends gain importance. The sibling bond seems to have primarily "instrumental" significance. This suggests that being a brother or sister remains significant primarily for the material demands we can make on the basis of a close blood tie. This limited utility suggests that with the increasing professionalization of society the sibling relationship will decline in importance.

We note with interest that spouses are distinguished from other types of people by the frequency they are thought about and are recipients of communication, but not by the frequency they are asked for advice. What type of discussion occurs between spouses? Is it restricted to problem-expression and the elicitation of sympathy?

TABLE 4–14

PERCENT WHO SEEK ADVICE FROM ANOTHER PERSON ON MONEY
AND ON FAMILY PROBLEMS FOR BLACKS

(By age of respondent and years in Milwaukee)

| Age | Years in Milwaukee | Percent who seek advice | | | |
| | | Money | | Family | |
		%	N	%	N
17–29	1–5	31	(71)	22	(71)
	6–15	15	(55)	18	(55)
	16 or more	53	(19)	50	(18)
30–39	1–5	25	(16)	19	(16)
	6–15	29	(68)	29	(68)
	16 or more	7	(28)	21	(28)
40 or over	1–5	36	(11)	27	(11)
	6–15	27	(55)	16	(55)
	16 or more	21	(76)	11	(76)

WHO SEEKS HELP

We found it difficult to understand what determined whether a person seeks advice from someone. First, we thought that perhaps such behavior is related to the severity of the problem, but we found no consistent relation between level of income and whether or not our respondents seek advice on money problems. Second, we thought that seeking advice might reflect the degree of personal resources our respondents have; so, we anticipated that better-educated people would more often solve their own problems; no support was found for this hypothesis. Similarly, we thought that working people would be more independent; no justification for this idea was found in our analysis.

It seemed almost natural to us that mobility would be related to seeking advice. It was reasoned that newcomers to a community would not have developed confidence in the people living in the new ciy, and therefore would not seek advice as often as less recent residents. For the entire sample of 623 women the percentage seeking advice among those who had lived one to five years in Milwaukee is 31 percent; for the rest of the sample it is 22 percent; contrary to our expectations, it appears that newcomers sought more advice.

Table 4-14 presents a more detailed analysis of the relation between mobility and seeking advice. It refers only to blacks; there were too few white cases for analysis. There is no consistent pattern in the table. Our basic conclusion must be that length of residence is unimportant; it does not seem to affect the way a woman solves her problem. There are, in retrospect, some obvious reasons why we are wrong about the significance of mobility: 1) Most people solve their own problems, whether stable or mobile; 2) Most advice is sought within family relationships, which seem able to endure in spite of mobility; and 3) It is possible that the lower class in a welfare society are accustomed to seeking advice via the service structure of impersonal, formal relationships, and so is not "at a loss" when in a new city.

There are, however, a few aspects of Table 4-14 worth noting. Among the seventeen to twenty-nine year-olds, for instance, an unusually high percentage of those who have lived in Milwaukee just about all their lives, i.e., sixteen or more years, seek advice. These life-long residents are probably just continuing a pattern of dependence developed while they lived with their parents. For older respondents, length of residence seems negatively related to seeking help. It is only among the young that long-term residents more often seek advice. Perhaps for young people mobility does what time away from the parental household eventually accomplishes anyway; either mobility or time can wean young people from their dependence on their parents.

Only the youngest age category has more than twenty newcomers. Within that category there is a considerable difference between newcomers and those that have lived in Milwaukee from six to fifteen years regarding the percent who seek help on money matters. (The life-time residents in this age category have already been discussed.) The difference is 16 percent for money problems, while it is only 6 percent for family problems. It is quite possible that newcomers experience pressing financial problems that the respondent herself must solve but for which purpose she lacks the necessary resources. Thus, newcomers might be forced to seek advice on financial problems because of their ignorance of the job market, the absence of friends they can temporarily borrow money from, or ignorance about existing welfare services. But there is no evidence suggesting a similar process for respondents over thirty. However, this could be due to the greater experience of older people, which minimizes the impact of mobility.

In the last paragraph we implicitly acknowledged that people may seek help but not advice. For instance, someone when in financial need may get a job; but, if asked whether she sought advice from someone, she might answer negatively; she knew what she had to do; she had to get a job. From the point of view of power, however, the company this woman now works for has some power over her. The company will, to some extent, shape this woman's life. The advice questions, then, are in no way a complete measure of power. What these questions do give is an indication of the respondents' awareness of being very dependent on another person or organization. To seek advice is 1) to be conscious of power, and 2) to be more dependent on another than is true if one simply works for a company or the like. When we seek advice on an important problem, we give the advisor more power over us than any single person from whom we receive help is likely to have. To seek advice is to give our lives into the hands of another. Few of our respondents did this.

Finally with regard to Table 4-14, there is a tendency among those thirty and over to seek less help if they have lived in Milwaukee sixteen or more years. The respondents thirty to thirty-nine years old, who have lived at least sixteen years in Milwaukee, stand out; only 7 percent seek advice on money problems. Overall in the table there is a tendency for older, long-term residents to seek less help. It is possible that there is such a thing as a settling-in, closing-out process. When people have resided in a city for a long time, they settle in, i.e., they learn what resources are available and how to use them; moreover, fewer problems might arise, because they have developed a set pattern of life acceptable to all in the family. At the same time, both because they are more able to handle their own problems, and because they have fewer problems, these older long-term residents seek less advice from others, thereby closing out others from their lives. These people settle in, and close out others.

These ideas relating mobility and advice-seeking are very tentative. The results in Table 4-14 are distinguished mainly by the absence of any overall pattern. It is quite possible that mobility has no effect on advice-seeking.

The main point of our discussion of power is how little social power seems to exist. As already noted the advice questions probably indicate only the existence of a conscious, high dependence on another. Still, the data do suggest that sociologists have too glibly assumed the interdependence of everyone. The "advice" questions suggest we should give more attention to self-involvement; our respondents appear more dependent on themselves than any other person. This phenomenon of self-involvement is poorly conceptualized in sociology and is usually not even admitted.[16]

THE MOTHER-CHILD RELATION

The most crucial involvement in American society is that between a mother and her children. We wanted to explore this relationship in particular. But how?

We are especially interested in the variables that affect the distribution of interpersonal knowledge in a complex society. Our interest in knowledge stems from previous attempts to study loneliness. We have defined loneliness as a sense of not being known as we perceive ourselves.[17] Loneliness is a truly modern problem, yet there is little significant research examining the distribution of interpersonal knowledge in the urban world.

Previous studies tell us little about what produces interpersonal knowledge: Luckey points to the variable of length of time a relationship has lasted and Jourard suggests that self-disclosure varies with the degree to which a person likes another (which process, however, is probably countered by the tendency to romanticize people we like).[18] All in all, however, we know little about the distribution of knowledge in our society or about the conditions that affect this distribution. The centrality of loneliness to an understanding of urban society suggests the desirability of research on this subject. Our work was meant to add a little more light on this basic problem.

Especially, we studied the mother's knowledge of her child. We did not have much time in the interview to spend on this subject, and we could interview only the mother. In addition, we had the problem of how to determine the accuracy of the mother's knowledge, since we could not interview the child. It seemed that we needed a question that was: 1) straight-forward and factual so that it would be a little difficult for the interviewee to lie; 2) that was about some significant aspect of the child's life, but 3) that was not central to the American concept of motherhood so that the respondent could admit ignorance without feeling guilty. We finally asked about the child's friend-a topic that we thought best fit our criteria. Each respondent was asked: "whom does (name of child) go around with most often?" This was asked for each living child the respondent had borne. In this section we shall only be concerned about the children living at home.

In coding the answers we used a number of categories that for present purposes we have reduced to three: gave a positive answer, said did not know, and no response. The interviewers had been specifically instructed to write in "D.K.", if the respondent said she did not know, but apparently many interviewers neglected this. We had the problem, then, of deciding what to do with the blank responses. Although we believed that in the majority of cases a blank meant ignorance, it also seemed that some interviewers did not always ask the question (specifically, at least one white interviewer appeared not to ask the question for children over twenty-one). In order to avoid arbitrary decisions, therefore, we excluded blanks from our analysis. Table 4-15 presents the percent of our respondents' children by their color and age whose mother did not know about their friend; since we believe that at least for those below twenty-one a blank also means ignorance we present in brackets the percentage of children for whom we have either a "D.K." or a blank response. The bracketed figure, we believe, expresses the degree of ignorance in K-3; however, for the remainder of our analysis we shall exclude the blanks, and consider only the cases that were coded "don't know" or for which we have a positive answer. We have used only cases in which the child is the respondent's by birth; other children, even if living with the respondent, are not considered.

As can be seen in Table 4-15 there are only minor differences associated with color; the white subsamples are small, but there is a consistent trend for the whites to be somewhat less ignorant. However, the important distinctions are between age aggregates. We found no significant difference between male and female children. Regardless of color or sex of child, as the child gets older fewer mothers know their children's friends.

76   SOLIDARITY IN A SLUM

Overall, less than a third of the children have a mother who said she did not know the child's friend. Given the fact, however, that this information is rather elementary, our results suggest a considerable amount of maternal ignorance in Kilbourntown.[19]

While considering the data about the friends of our respondents' children, we were struck by the infrequency of these children having siblings as their friends. Table 4-16 shows how many mothers reported that their children's friends were siblings and the frequency the mothers said simply "the family" in response to the question about their children's friend. Among very young children there is a high degree of sibling solidarity, but this falls off quickly as the child's age increases. According to the mothers' reports, then, sibling solidarity seems inconsequential once children are old enough to go about the neighborhood on their own. This topic is worth further investigation. Why is it that young people who eat and sleep together seem not to "pal around" together? An investigation of this would shed light on such topics as the incest taboo and the nature of friendship and love.

TABLE 4–15

PERCENT OF CHILDREN WHOSE FRIEND IS NOT KNOWN
BY MOTHER

| Age of child | Color (By age of child and color of child) | | | |
| | White | | Black | |
	%	N	%	N
0–4	11	(19)	17	(184)
5–6	17	(18)	18	(117)
7–13	11	(80)[23%][1]	18	(355)[26%]
14–18	26	(31)[36%]	32	(135)[35%]
19–21	31	(13)[48%]	35	(23)[40%]
22 plus	58	(12)	65	(26)
No response	—	(5)	—	(19)
		(178[2])		(859[3])

1. In brackets are the percentages of total cases for a category that were either left blank by the interviewer or in which the mother said she did not know her child's friend; these percentages are given only for the age aggregates for which a blank was most likely to represent ignorance. Before we grouped the children we examined ignorance by year of age. The aggregates we used, in our opinion, reflect either "natural" groupings (our breaking points represent significant changes in ignorance) or common sense (e.g., separation of 0–6 years from 7–13).

2. Because of blanks we had to exclude thirty eight cases.

3. Because of blanks we had to exclude seventy nine cases.

TABLE 4–16

PERCENT OF REFERENCES TO "FAMILY" OR A SIBLING AS BEING CHILD'S FRIEND

(By age of child and color of respondent)

Age of child	Percent "family"[1]				Percent sibling				Total	
	White		Black		White		Black		White	Black
	%	N	%	N	%	N	%	N	%	%
0–4	5	(19)	8	(184)	16	(19)	28	(184)	21	36
5–6	0	(18)	6	(117)	0	(18)	9	(117)	0	15
7–13	0	(80)	3	(355)	0	(80)	4	(355)	0	7
14–18	0	(31)	1	(135)	0	(31)	1	(135)	0	2
19–21	0	(13)	0	(23)	0	(13)	9	(23)	0	9
22 plus	0	(12)	4	(26)	0	(12)	0	(26)	0	4

1. I.e. the percent of cases in which the mothers responded to the questions about their children's friends by saying "the family."

In light of the small subsample sizes among the whites the white-black differences in Table 4-16 seem too small to comment on.

It is important to remember that in this discussion of mothers' ignorance the tables are based on the child as the unit of analysis. This means that the number of mothers being discussed is always smaller than the number of cases, i.e., children, reported in the following tables.

IGNORANCE AMONG WHITES

Although there are relatively few data on white children, a clear pattern emerges.

The mothers' age is significantly related to ignorance—the older the mothers are, the less often they know their childrens' friends. Similarly, separated white mothers more often are ignorant than either divorced or married ones. Table 4-17 shows the percent of children whose friend is not known by the mother, according to her marital status and age. Considering only the married mothers, the effect of a mother's age can be seen; considering only the young mothers, the effect of marital status can be seen. Clearly, being separated and being forty or more in age is associated with ignorance.

It is possible that the mother's age is not itself important and that the association of ignorance with older women is due to the fact that older children are less well known. In Table 4-18 the separate effect of child's age and mother's age can be seen. Among the children between the ages of nine and thirteen we can see the effect of mother's age, while a consideration of children

TABLE 4–17

MARITAL STATUS, MOTHER'S AGE, AND PERCENT OF CHILDREN
WHOSE FRIEND IS "NOT" KNOWN BY MOTHER

(For whites only)

Marital status[1]	Mother's age			
	20–39 years		40–78 years	
	%	N	%	N
Married	3	(66)	22	(59)
Divorced	0	(12)	–	(3)
Separated	42	(19)	–	(9)[2]

1. There are too few "never married" and "widowed" cases to justify presentation of these categories.

2. The percentage is 67 percent.

whose mothers are forty or more shows a jump in ignorance for children nineteen or more years of age. If we compare Tables 4-15 and 4-18, it can be seen that there is an increase in maternal ignorance for children fourteen to eighteen years old in the former table but not in the latter. In Table 4-18 mother's age is controlled; the absence of an increase in ignorance among the fourteen to eighteen years olds in this table suggests that the increase found in Table 4-15 for children of this age is due to these children's having older

TABLE 4–18

AGE OF CHILD, MOTHER'S AGE AND PERCENT OF CHILDREN
WHOSE FRIEND IS NOT KNOWN BY MOTHER

(For married whites only.)

Marital status[1]	Age of child[2]	Mother's age			
		20–39 years		40 plus	
		%	N	%	N
Married	7–13	0	(37)	17	(18)
	14–18	–	(6)[3]	19	(16)
	19 plus	–	(2)	41	(17)

1. There are too few cases of divorced or separated status to analyze.

2. There are too few cases of children below seven years to analyze.

3. There is one case of ignorance.

TABLE 4–19

WORK STATUS OF MOTHER, SOURCE OF INCOME FOR FAMILY, AND
PERCENT OF CHILDREN WHOSE FRIEND IS NOT KNOWN
BY MOTHER

	(For whites)							
	Main source of income for family							
Respondent's work status	*Job*		*Social Security*		*Welfare*		*Other*	
	%	N	%	N	%	N	%	N
Full-time	0	(17)	—	(1)	—	(1)	—	(0)
Part-time	—	(2)	—	(0)	—	(0)	—	(2)
Unemployed	—	(0)	—	(0)	—	(6)	—	(7)
Retired	—	(3)	—	(2)	—	(0)	—	(0)
Not looking	15	(86)	—	(4)	37	(32)	—	(4)

mothers and is not due to any significant developments in the child's way of life in mid-adolescence. But the data in Table 4-18 do support the idea that older children, i.e., adult children, are less known by their mothers.

Maternal ignorance of their children's friends, then, is associated with living in a separated home, being an older child, and having an older mother.

But these characteristics present only part of the picture. Before we interpret our results we must get a more complete overview of the white mothers who are ignorant of their children. Ignorance is also associated with having only a grade school or no education. This variable is independent of age, i.e., among both young and old mothers little education tends to mean ignorance. Because of our small subsamples it is impossible to meaningfully subdivide our tables further. We can not determine the specific variables that are most important in producing ignorance. What we can do, however, is to present a composite profile of white ignorant mothers. So far, then, ignorance of children's friends is associated with mothers who are: older, less educated (no more then eight years of schooling), and separated from their spouses.

Table 4-19 presents data on the relation between economic factors and ignorance. One obvious conclusion is that working does not seem to produce ignorance. On the contrary ignorance is associated with not looking for a job, but especially with being welfare recipients. The results of this table remain the same when age of child is controlled. (It should be noted, however, that only one child over 19 lives in a home dependent on welfare; the ignorance associated with older children cannot be explained by the attitude of welfare mothers.) There are relatively few cases of poverty among our whites; on the

TABLE 4–20

ABSENCE OF RESPONSE TO THE "PROUD" QUESTION, AS OF CHILD,
AND PERCENT OF CHILDREN WHOSE FRIEND IS NOT KNOWN
BY MOTHER

	(For whites)			
Age of child[1]	Gave some answer to "proud" question		No answer[2]	
	%	N	%	N
7–13	5	(60)	35	(17)
14–18	0	(20)	80	(10)

1. There are too few cases in the other age ranges to analyze.

2. I.e. did not acknowledge pride in any phenomenon in response to the "proud" question.

basis of what information we do have there appears to be no relation between poverty and ignorance. Working, then, is associated with knowledge; being on welfare with maternal ignorance.

If we pool our information, the image of the ignorant mother that emerges is of a woman over forty, with little formal education, separated from her husband, and living on welfare. The statistical tools available to us did not allow us to determine the relative significance of each of these variables. We suggest, however, that there are two distinct processes represented in our data: 1) maternal ageing—as mothers get old, they lose interest in their children, perhaps because they have become interested in other things, or because they have already begun to disengage or because they have become disillusioned with family life; and 2) anomic white women gravitate to the slum; these ignorant mothers seem to be societal failures—they failed to go beyond elementary school, are separated (or were deserted) rather than divorced, and they fail to support themselves; we suggest that such women are anomic, i.e., without hope of success of any kind. In Table 4-20 we show the relation between ignorance and pride, as indicated by the previously discussed "proud" question. Clearly, for the age aggregates reported (and, although the numbers are small, the same results occur for the children aged five to six), ignorance is associated with the absence of pride on the part of the mother. It does not seem far-fetched to interpret these data to mean that at times ignorant mothers are hopeless women. It should be emphasized, however, that there seem to be two hypotheses about ignorance worth pursuing-one relates ignorance to maternal ageing, the other to anomie associated with little education, separation, and living on welfare. It is possible, of course, that both the disillusionment that comes with ageing and the hopelessness that comes from repeated social

TABLE 4–21

AGE OF CHILD, MARITAL STATUS, AND AGE OF MOTHER, AND
PERCENT OF CHILDREN WHOSE FRIEND IS NOT KNOWN
BY MOTHER

(For blacks)

	Marital status and age of mother					
	Married			Separated		
Age of Child	20–29	30–39	Over 39	20–29	30–39	Over 39
	% N	% N	% N	% N	% N	% N
5–6	11 (43)	29 (32)	— (2)	6 (17)	— (7)	— (4)
7–13	5 (53)	24 (154)	19 (23)	3 (32)	24 (33)	37 (19)
14–18	— (0)	32 (69)	41 (22)	— (0)	10 (10)	33 (18)

failures lead to anomie, which produces mothers ignorant of children's friends.

However, this analysis does not explain the ignorance found about the friends of the older children living at home. The variables we have discussed are unable to explain the large number of mothers who were ignorant of the friends of their children who were nineteen or over. It is possible that older children who remain at home seek ways to establish that although still at home they are now adults and no longer children. One way to do this, perhaps, is to keep parents ignorant of leisure time associates and activities. This could be a way of asserting one's independence of the family, and thereby one's adult status.

MATERNAL IGNORANCE AMONG BLACKS

Just as ignorant white mothers perfectly fit our stereotype of the slum family, so black ignorant mothers with equal clarity do not fit this pattern. Table 4-17 contains data showing that among whites ignorance is associated with mothers being separated and being older. Table 4-21 contains data for the black sample relating child's age, mother's marital status, mother's age, and ignorance. Children below five are excluded, because it could be argued that it is not meaningful to ask about the best friend of such a young child (although it should be remembered that the actual question asked the respondent about the person her child went around with most often). Children nineteen and over are excluded, because for whites the variables of mother's age and marital status are not significant in explaining ignorance about these older children living at home; moreover, there are so few adult children living at home that detailed analyses on this subsample are not possible.

TABLE 4–22

PERCENT OF CHILDREN WHOSE FRIEND IS NOT KNOWN BY
MOTHER: BY AGE OF CHILD AND AGE OF MOTHER

	(For blacks)						
	Age of mother						
Age of child	17–19		20–29		30–39		40 or over
	% N		% N		% N		% N
0–6	— (2)		12 (189)		26 (95)		9 (11)
7–13	— (0)		6 (94)		23 (209)		22 (51)
14–18	— (0)		— (0)		30 (85)		34 (47)

Contrary to what is true for whites, there is no consistent difference between the children with married mothers and those with separated mothers among black respondents. Holding age of mother and of child constant, there are six possible comparisons of married and separated cases in Table 4-21. In four of these comparisons the married mothers are more ignorant, in one comparison married and separated mothers are the same, and in one comparison the separated mothers are more ignorant. No matter how the data were analyzed, married women tended to be more ignorant than separated ones. However, the data were not completely consistent, as in Table 4-21; sometimes separated mothers were more ignorant. These inconsistencies have led us to reject marital status as an important variable for understanding the distribution of knowledge among black people.

Table 4-21 does suggest that a mother's age is important. The mothers in their twenties are dramatically less ignorant. Table 4-22 presents the data on mother's age a little more clearly. Young mothers definitely are less ignorant. An exception to the overall pattern of the table is the case of very young children with mothers forty or more years old; there the percentage is only 9 percent; however,there are only eleven children in this category. It is possible, of course, that older women who have very young children represent a distinct type of person; to give birth at such a relatively advanced age might indicate real love of children or at least dedication to the role of mother. Overall, however, there is a major difference between mothers in their twenties and all others. There is also a tendency for ignorance to increase as the child's age increases, especially among children whose mother is forty or more.

Why do these young mothers seem to know more? Among the whites, also, mother's age is significant; the small number of cases we have prevents reaching any firm conclusion about how similar the white mothers in their

TABLE 4–23

PERCENT OF CHILDREN WHOSE FRIEND IS NOT KNOWN BY MOTHER BY WORK STATUS OF MOTHER AND SOURCE OF INCOME FOR FAMILY

(For blacks)

Respondent's work status	Main source of income for family							
	Job		Social security		Welfare		Other[1]	
	%	N	%	N	%	N	%	N
Full-time work	22	(167)	—	(2)	—	(2)	—	(7)
Part-time work	29	(79)	—	(1)	—	(7)	—	(2)
Unemployed	13	(54)	—	(0)	6	(43)	—	(13)
Retired	—	(8)	—	(0)	—	(3)	—	(0)
Not looking	23	(274)	48	(16)	25	(131)	—	(50)

1. This category is not analyzed, because it refers to a variety of sources of income.

twenties are to those in their thirties, but it does seem that for whites the critical difference is between those below forty and those above forty. The fact that the critical age seems to be thirty for blacks and forty for whites confuses the issue. There is a definite indication, however, that something happens to both whites and blacks as they grow old that turns their attention away from children, regardless of the child's age. This seems to occur earlier for blacks. Is this due to a general decline of interest in life? Is it due to an increase in self-involvement? Is it due to a shift of involvement to other people? Is it due to a growing disillusionment with life, which hits black women at an earlier age?

Are black mothers on welfare more ignorant than those whose families are supported by income from a job? The answer is clearly "no." In Table 4-23 ignorance is not associated with either the work status of the respondent or the main source of family income. Among women neither working nor looking for a job, there is only a 2 percent difference between those whose source of income is from a job (usually the spouse's) and those whose source of income is welfare.

Clearly, we cannot evaluate white and black families by the same criteria. At least as far as our sample is concerned, the assumption that separation and living on welfare are signs of poor home life may have some validity for whites, although even among the whites neither a majority of children on welfare nor a majority from separated homes have ignorant mothers, but such an assumption seems useless for black families. Neither source of income nor marital

TABLE 4-24

PERCENT OF CHILDREN WHOSE FRIEND IS NOT KNOWN BY MOTHER BY AGE OF CHILD AND WORK STATUS OF MOTHER

(For blacks)[1]

			Work status			
				Working full-time		
Age of child	Not working		Including nights and/or weekends		Not including nights or weekends	
	%	N	%	N	%	N
0–4	17	(116)	20	(15)	—	(8)
5–6	19	(72)	9	(11)	9	(11)
7–13	22	(183)	17	(42)	20	(41)
14–18	34	(65)	30	(10)	29	(14)

1. Because of too few cases we did not include children nineteen or over, (N=49).

status, on the basis of our data, are good indicators of the quality of family relations. Of course, studies of other aspects of family life may lead to different conclusions about the relation between welfare and separation and poor home life.

Nor is the reason for the failure of these assumptions about the meaning of being on welfare or of being separated due to the blacks' having a uniformly high percentage of ignorant mothers regardless of marital or income status. Compare Tables 4-19 and 4-23. Considering the welfare families, there is more ignorance among the whites than the blacks.

The fact seems to be that marital status and source of income are not indicators of maternal ignorance of children's friends among black mothers.

Looking again at Table 4-23 the only really high percentage of ignorance occurs for children whose mothers are on social security. But, of course, these would be adult children for whom ignorance is expected. More difficult to explain is why unemployed mothers seem not to be ignorant regardless of whether income is from either a job or welfare. We do not know why this is true.

Because so much is made of economic determinants in analyzing human behavior, we tried to delve deeper into the economic life of our black respondents. As can be seen in table 4-24, holding the child's age constant, whether a black woman works and whether she works on nights or weekends makes little difference. It is true that working mothers of children five to six years old appear somewhat less ignorant than mothers not working, but the subsample sizes are small. Overall, work status seems of little importance in itself.

THE HOUSEHOLD AND FAMILY

TABLE 4–25

PERCENT OF CHILDREN WHOSE FRIEND IS NOT KNOWN BY
MOTHER: BY SOURCE OF INCOME FOR FAMILY, AGE OF CHILD,
AND POVERTY

	(For blacks)						
	Children 0–13				Children 14–18		
Source of income	Poverty		Non-Poverty		Poverty		Non-Poverty	
	%	N	%	N	%	N	%	N
Job	21	(154)	15	(224)	38	(32)	31	(51)
Welfare	24	(92)	8	(36)	25	(16)	—	(8)

Table 4-25 relates source of income and poverty to ignorance; because age fourteen seems to be a breaking point in the career of a child, at least regarding the mother's knowledge, we divided the children into two aggregates: thirteen and younger, and fourteen to eighteen. In general being poverty-stricken seems slightly related to ignorance; for the younger children whose mothers are on welfare the effect of not being in poverty is quite substantial. However, there are only thirty-six cases of young children who are on welfare but not in poverty. If we consider only young children from homes dependent on a job, there is only a difference of 6 percent between those below the poverty line and those above it; what makes this comparison important is the large number of cases. Poverty, then, seems unrelated to ignorance.

We also investigated the effects of unemployment. Holding constant both mothers' and children's ages as well as level of income, and using only families whose main source of income is a job, we compared the knowledge of mothers from families in which the breadwinner has not been unemployed or laid off the previous year with those from families in which the breadwinner has experienced one or more weeks of loss of regular income. Unemployment shows no consistent effect, although there is a tendency in families earning $4,000 or more for greater ignorance to occur when the breadwinner has been unemployed or laid off. Yet no such relation appears among the poorer families. Too few cases prevented further analysis. On the whole, the economic variables are not very powerful predictors of ignorance.

Because we thought that this failure might be due to a lack of control for non-economic variables, we further analyzed our data on work status and source of income, holding constant the mothers' and children's ages. Table 4-26 presents the results. We excluded children less than five years old from our analysis, because it does not seem as meaningful to talk about friends at this age. Behavior is not as stable. When both mother and child are young, economic variables are unimportant, except that again unemployed mothers are low in ignorance. For middle-aged mothers with young children, unemployment again means knowledge, while not looking for work and relying on a breadwinner with a job is associated with ignorance. It is difficult to analyze the effects of economic variables on older children, because the different combinations have low frequencies; however, the pattern seems similar to that for younger children with mothers the same age, except for the relatively high ignorance of part-time workers. What is most interesting about Table 4-26 is the suggestive evidence that ignorance is associated with children whose mothers are not looking for a job but are dependent on some working member of the family. We expected the reverse. For mothers thirty or more, ignorance is highest among the "fat cats."

In an analysis not reported in detail because the frequencies of many combinations of the variables were too small to justify comment, we compared children in families with an annual income below $4,000 with children in families whose income was $4,000 or more. Mother's age and child's age were

TABLE 4–26

PERCENT OF CHILDREN WHOSE FRIEND IS NOT KNOWN BY MOTHER: BY MOTHER'S AGE, CHILD'S AGE, WORK STATUS OF MOTHER, AND SOURCE OF INCOME FOR FAMILY

| | | | Source of income | | | |
| | | | Job | | Welfare | |
Mother's age	Child's age	Mother's work status	%	N	%	N
16–29	5–13	Full-time job	11	(35)	—	(0)
		Part-time job	—	(4)	—	(0)
		Unemployed	—	(7)	0	(11)
		Not looking	7	(60)	10	(30)
30 plus	5–13	Full-time job	16	(69)	—	(1)
		Part-time job	18	(28)	—	(4)
		Unemployed	4	(24)	8	(13)
		Not looking	32	(85)	20	(46)
30 plus	14–18	Full-time job	23	(22)	—	(1)
		Part-time job	35	(26)	—	(3)
		Unemployed	—	(9)	—	(1)
		Not looking	40	(35)	30	(20)

(For blacks)[1]

1. In three cases mother was retired, and these are not reported. Children less than five or more than eighteen are excluded from this table. Not reported are cases having sources of income other than job or welfare.

TABLE 4–27

PERCENT OF CHILDREN WHOSE FRIEND IS NOT KNOWN BY MOTHER: BY MOTHER'S AGE, CHILD'S AGE, WORK STATUS OF MOTHER, AND PRIDE

			(For blacks)			
Mother's age	Child's age	Work status	Proud of something		Proud of nothing	
			%	N	%	N
17–29	5–13	Works full-time	7	(27)	—	(8)
		Works part-time	—	(2)	—	(2)
		Unemployed	7	(15)	—	(3)
		Not looking	7	(75)	11	(28)
30–39	5–13	Works full-time	14	(36)	8	(13)
		Works part-time	—	(8)	38	(21)
		Unemployed	3	(38)	—	(7)
		Not looking	21	(84)	56	(43)

[Other subsamples are too small for analysis.]

held constant. There was one significant finding worth reporting. There were fifty-nine children between the ages of five and thirteen whose mothers were thirty or more and whose family income from a job was $4,000 or more. The ignorance-percentage for this category was 41 percent, by far the highest percentage found in that analysis. This result supports the "fat cat" theory; among the black mothers ignorance is highest among the older, relatively well-off families.

To get some indication of the mother's attitude we performed an analysis similar to that in Table 4-25, except that we dropped the variable "source of income" and replaced it with whether the respondent had given a positive answer to the "proud" question. The results are in Table 4-27. As can be seen, pride is insignificant for the children of young mothers. However, among the older mothers not interested in working, there is a difference of 35 percent between those who said they were proud of something and those that did not. The ignorant "fat cats" seem to be prideless. Ideally, of course, we should further subdivide Table 4-27 by income, but there are not enough cases to do this. It seems, however, that ignorance is associated with a mother who is: thirty or more years old, not looking for work, being supported by a breadwinner who has a job, in a family with an income of $4,000 or more a year, yet proud of nothing.

Ignorance seems associated with a combination of relative success and disillusionment. Perhaps it is among the relatively prosperous "fat cats" in black America that white racism takes its heaviest toll. It is conceivable that the older black women with some money have had to endure more frustrations resulting from the prejudice and discrimination existing in American society than poorer black women. In reaction to this these less poverty-stricken women may cease to care; they may cease to be interested in their environment, including their children. Perhaps the reason, then, why 'fat cats" tend to be ignorant of their child's friend is because they have suffered more disillusionment resulting from their encounters with white racism. Of course, this line of reasoning is only conjecture.

Considering all the analysis done on economic variables, the main conclusion is that economic conditions do not seem to significantly affect interpersonal understanding in the mother-child relationship among black people. In fact, such conditions seem totally inconsequential for black mothers in their twenties. For the older women two lines of analysis seem worth following-up. First, interpersonal knowledge seems associated with being unemployed. This label was applied to a jobless respondent if she said she was looking for a job when asked about her work status. It does not seem possible that the economic condition of being unemployed itself produces more knowledgeable mothers. There must be some non-economic characteristic associated with being unemployed in a place like Kilbourtown that accounts for this association of unemployment with knowledge. Second, some evidence was found supporting a "fat cat" theory.

But perhaps our most important conclusion is that maternal ignorance of their children's friends is associated with quite different conditions for whites and blacks. For the former, ignorance means separation and being on welfare. Neither of these conditions is indicative of ignorance in the black sample. In fact, economic conditions in general do not seem to be important determinants of black maternal ignorance. Of course, our comments are based only on a single question, which, however, was about an important area in a child's life.

FAMILY STRUCTURE AND IGNORANCE AMONG BLACK FAMILIES

Because there are relatively few whites in Kilbourntown, this section discusses only the black families. The question we are interested in is whether the kind of people living in a household influences the distribution of understanding in a family.

We have already concluded that there is no consistent relation between marital status and ignorance; moreover, an analysis by age of child that compared families with husbands and those without showed no relation between ignorance and the presence of a husband in a home. We thought that spacing might be significant; we reasoned that the closer children were in age, the more likely the mother might be forced to spread her attention, with the result that

TABLE 4–28

CHILD-SPACING AND PERCENT OF CHILDREN WHOSE FRIEND IS NOT KNOWN BY MOTHER

(For blacks)[1]

Spacing	Percent ignorant	
	%	N
No child within one year	22	(482)
One child a year apart— sibling older	25	(278)
One child a year apart— sibling younger	28	(268)
Two children within a year	26	(109)

1. Only children seven, eight, eleven, twelve, and fifteen years of age are included in this table.

she would know her children less well. We analyzed data only about children seven, eight, eleven, twelve and fifteen years of age. We compared children with no sibling within one year of them with those that had one sibling within a year with those that had two siblings within a year of age. The results are presented in Table 4-28 for ages, which we analyzed, combined; separate analyses for each age yielded data similar to that in Table 4-28. Obviously, child-density as we have measured it is not related to ignorance.

We also thought that the number of children under six years might be critical, because of the attention they require; no significance was found.

We also investigated family size. We were guided by the simple idea that the more people someone is related to, the less interest there is to invest in any one object. We used several ways of getting at size, but finally concentrated on the number of children. Comparing the results obtained (holding constant the child's age) by relating ignorance first with household family size and then with the number of the respondent's own children living at home and sixteen or under, we found that: 1) the two tables revealed the same pattern of results for children below fourteen; 2) the second measure, based only on the number of children, seemed more sensitive for those fourteen to eighteen. In light of the fact that household family size seemed less significant, and because the same household size could mean quite different household compositions, we decided to concentrate our analysis on the number of children.

Table 4-29 shows the effect of number of children at home on ignorance, holding constant mother's age. We used only the number of children at home who were sixteen years of age or under; this age range was used mainly because of the manner in which we coded our material. There is some meaning to this category, however; children sixteen or less are still highly dependent on the

TABLE 4-29

PERCENT OF CHILDREN WHOSE FRIEND IS NOT KNOWN BY
MOTHER: BY MOTHER'S AGE, CHILD'S AGE, AND NUMBER OF
RESPONDENT'S OWN CHILDREN SIXTEEN OR LESS LIVING AT HOME

(For blacks)

Age of mother	Age of child	Number of own children 16 or less living at home							
		1–2		*3–5*		*6–8*		*9 plus*	
		%	N	%	N	%	N	%	N
17–29	5–13	16	(19)	8	(97)	10	(41)	—	(0)
30–39	5–13	16	(19)	13	(84)	31	(32)	27	(33)
	14–18	—	(5)	7	(29)	48	(31)	31	(13)
40–85	5–13	38	(16)	17	(30)	—	(8)	—	(0)
	14–18	50	(16)	27	(22)	—	(2)	—	(0)

mothers; after sixteen, children begin to take on adult status, especially in the black community. Our measure of household composition, then, refers only to the number of nonadult children at home.

Because of the necessity to hold constant both mother's age as well as child's age some of the cell frequencies in Table 4-29 are small. The data do suggest, however, that mothers are ignorant least often not in the smallest families but in those with three to five children at home. Reading across the table this family size consistently has the least ignorance. For young mothers, i.e., those between seventeen and twenty-nine years of age, the differences are rather small; young mothers seem to know their child's friend no matter what. Also, the difference between families of one to two children and families with three to five children is rather small (3 percent) for mothers in their thirties when the children are five to thirteen years old. Overall, however, maternal ignorance is least in families with three to five children, and is highest when there are more than five children at home.

Although not reported here, different family sizes were compared holding constant the presence of pride in something, and there was still a tendency for mothers with three to five dependent children at home to most often know their child's friend.

Why does there seem to be a curvilinear relation between the number of dependent children at home and the percentage of ignorant mothers? The association of knowledge with three to five dependent children at home could be explained by saying that this is enough children so that the mother is forced to devote her time and interest to the house, but not so many that her interest is overstretched. This reasoning, however, does not explain why family size is generally not very significant for young mothers. It would seem realistic to assume that young women are affected by the cultural value attached to motherhood; for young women there is probably a tendency to idealize motherhood and its rewards. But as women gain experience as mothers, it is possible that they become more realistic, and see both the frustrations as well as rewards of having children. We suggest that when this disillusionment with an idealized motherhood sets in, the number of children becomes an important consideration for the development of maternal understanding. If, at this time, there are few children, mothers might feel free to become deeply involved in other relationships and tend to become ignorant of their children's lives. On the other hand, if, at the time of disillusionment, women have many children, (i.e., five or more), they are still likely to seek to develop some new involvement not centering on the children, and this involvement plus all the demands of a large family will overstretch their interest and lead to maternal ignorance.

To summarize: we have tried to uncover some of the conditions that affect the distribution of interpersonal knowledge. We suggest that the following ideas are worth more exploration: 1) Parents tend to be ignorant about the personal life of adult children at home; adult children might feel it is necessary to maintain a private life as a way of symbolizing their status as adults, especially when they continue to live with their parents; 2) Young mothers more often know about their children than old ones, although "young" means below forty for whites but below thirty for blacks; the lack of ignorance among young mothers might be due to their romantic ideas about motherhood with the result that they devote much time and attention to the family; however, this does not explain why the meaning of "young" seems different for whites and blacks; 3) At least for the black respondents (there were too few white mothers to analyze) family density does not seem to affect the distribution of knowledge in the family, but family size does; ignorance occurs least often when there are three to five dependent children at home; it was suggested that this number draws the mother's interest to the family without overstretching it; 4) Among whites, maternal ignorance seems to be part of a generally anomic life; ignorant mothers are separated, uneducated, living on welfare, and lacking in pride; ignorant white mothers seem to be people uninterested in anything; 5) The pattern associated with ignorance is quite different among the black respondents; ignorant mothers are not looking for work, are dependent on a breadwinner with a job, live in a family making $4,000 or more, but are proud of nothing. The association of ignorance and no pride is common to both whites and blacks, but the social context is quite different. Among whites pridelessness seems associated with social failure, while among blacks it seems to be part of a syndrome of variables that indicate worldly success. To explain this difference we presented the "fat cat" theory, which suggests that white racism tends to breed disillusionment among the more leisured more economically secure black women, thus bringing about the association of modest success and maternal ignorance of their children's friends.

We checked the relation between mobility and ignorance. Holding constant the age both of the mother and of the child, no relation was found between "years at present address" and ignorance. Holding constant the child's age, we also investigated the relation between "the number of moves in the last five years" and ignorance; the data suggest that frequent moving might be significant for children fourteen to eighteen years old; 23 percent of these children in families that have not moved or have moved only once in the last five years (N=48) have ignorant mothers, while 42 percent of the children have ignorant mothers in families that have moved two or more times (N=52). There was no relation between "number of towns and cities lived in" and ignorance. Overall, mobility seemed insignificant.

THE NATURAL HISTORY OF FAMILY INVOLVEMENT

Many sociologists working on the family have stressed the importance of a developmental perspective; there are events of sociological significance that occur in almost every family in a set sequence; the developmental approach suggests the question: what are the effects on family life of passing through each step in the sequence?

Reuben Hill has suggested the following developmental description of the family:

> Employing these...sets of readily available data of numbers of positions in the family, age composition of the family, and employment status of the father, several stages of the family life span can be differentiated, each representing a distinctive role complex, as follows: Stage I Establishment (newly married, childless); II New Parents (infant-3 years); III Preschool Family (Child 3-6 years and possibly younger siblings); IV School-Age Family (oldest child 6-12 years, possibly younger siblings); V Family with adolescent (oldest 13-19, possibly younger siblings); VI Family with Young Adult (oldest 20 or more, until first child leaves home); VII Family as Launching Center (from departure of first to last child); VIII Postparental Family, The Middle Years (after children have left home until father retires); IX Aging Family (after retirement of father.)[20]

There are problems with using this framework for analyzing family development. First there is a minor problem; stage II seems to assume that a second child does not come along until the first one is three years old. Second, this set of stages must be received as tentative because we can not be sure that it isolates the most important variables for understanding family life; for example, stages II-VI are based entirely on the age of the oldest child irrespective of the age and sex and total number of other children; this is obviously inadequate; for example, our analysis of maternal ignorance suggests the importance of the number of children present in the household. Similarly, stages VI-VIII do not take into account the order in which children leave the home or the reasons for leaving or the type of child leaving, e.g., the effect is no doubt different if a daughter leaves home than if a son does. Moreover, Hill's analysis does not allow for the effect of wives entering and leaving the work force.

It might be objected that the idea of a "stage" approach is all wrong. The world is made up of processes; talking about "stages" seems to unduly harden the world. There is justification for this criticism to the extent that all of life cannot be viewed as a series of stages; for example, the tendency of married couples to become disillusioned over time with their marriage seems better described as a continual, gradual process than as a series of stages. There might be a point of recognition that could be called "The Stage of Consciously Recognized Disillusion," but for some even the recognition is a slow, gradual process. To talk about stages in regard to this process of disillusionment seems to misrepresent reality. On the other hand, the family does experience discontinuity, and this is what the "stage" approach emphasizes. One day there are no children, the next day the dyad is a triad; one day the man is working, the next day he is retired. Of course it is true that humans are capable of preparing for these events. It may be asked, therefore, if there really is a significant difference between the process of disillusionment and the transition from work to retirement? There does seem to be a difference; in the former case adjustment often precedes the shock of recognition, i.e., we begin changing our lives before we fully realize how disillusioned we are; on the other hand, the shock of retirement hits before we can adjust to it. The concept of stage, therefore seems appropriate for certain events in family development.

Having said this, it must also be acknowledged that no one has proved that his list of stages completely represents all the key moments in the development of family life. For example, disillusionment with spouse might occur quite independently of the appearance of the various stages suggested by Hill. His suggested discontinuous events or stages are not equally significant for all familial characteristics.

A major weakness of our research was our failure to relate family involvement to the various stages in family development as enunciated, for instance, by Hill. To some extent we approximated them, but we could have tested the significance of each stage for involvement; unfortunately, we did not do this. Like many other studies, we talk about development, even though we have studied not the same families over time, but different families at different points of development; any statement about the development of involvement, then, can only be tentative. Our analysis, however, does suggest some comments about a natural history of involvement, which are worth future exploration.

Maternal involvement with children seems to follow this pattern. Stage

I—Child is zero to four years of age: *high* involvement based on the need of young children for a great deal of attention (Note the high percentage of infants who are thought about; see Table 4-4); Stage II—Child is five to sixteen: *moderate* involvement based on mother's dominance of the child (As children grow up they are less often thought about, and rarely do parents use children in this age range as confidants; however, mothers do know about the lives of these children, indicating high maternal dominance; See Tables 4-4, 4-7, and 4-15.); Stage III—Child is a young adult: *moderate* involvement based on the exchange of confidences (The adult child is more likely to be thought about and to be used as a confidant, but mothers seem to know less about their adult children; it should be noted that the comments about maternal ignorance of adult children are based only on the study of adult children living at home); Stage IV—Child ages, and parents enter old age: *high* involvement due to the greater concentration of involvement by parents in parent-child relations (See column 2 in Table 4-1; as can be seen in this table, whites generally concentrate their involvement on their children more than blacks. But what we are interested in is that for both blacks and whites, as the parents age, there is a jump in the importance of children in their fantasy life;[21] it is the "jump" that interests us here. We are assuming that, because the concentration of involvement increases, the actual degree of parental involvement with their children increases.)

This analysis suggests the need to investigate the significance of changes in degree of involvement within the same relationship. For instance, what is the effect of changing from high to moderate to high involvement? Will the first experience of high involvement be the same as the second? Will the fact of having experienced a decline in involvement affect children's attitude toward an increase of involvement when parents reach old age? Equally interesting to investigate are the consequences of a change in the basis of involvement from power to knowledge.

Our comments on the natural history of involvement are based on the age of the individual child, while Hill's stages are, for the most part, based on the age of the oldest child in the family. In our analysis of maternal ignorance, we did control for various structural variables, such as number of children nineteen and over in a family, number of children six years of age or less, the spacing of children, and the number of dependent children at home. Only the last variable seemed related to mother's ignorance of her child's life. On the basis of the many failures we had in using structural variables it seems doubtful to us that the age of the oldest child itself, i.e., independent of the age of the individual child we are studying, could be very significant. The value of Hill's work is that it makes us think in terms of structural effects on individual relationships; such effects need more attention in sociology. But on the basis of our work we would suggest that a structural analysis should center not on the age of the oldest child but on the number of dependent children at home. Starting with this variable sociologists can then devise more complicated structural types that make use of information on the age and sex-distribution of those children as well as the age of the parents.

FINAL COMMENT

I am struck by the hints uncovered in the research about how cut-off our respondents are. Consider these facts: 1) Most of the respondents report seeking help with their problems from no one; they solve their own problems. 2) About a third of the respondents said they do not discuss their personal problems with the people they think about. 3) About one-quarter of the children have mothers who said they did not know the person their children went around with most often. These facts suggest an aggregate of people who are in the world but not of it, of people who keep their problems to themselves —or rather, people who keep their selves to themselves. To talk of isolated people is, however, inaccurate. Our respondents work and raise families. As physical entities the women we studied are involved with their environment, but as human beings they seem alienated. They do what is necessary. Perhaps what we are searching for is the distinction between necessary and voluntary involvement. At least let us suggest that a measure of the purely voluntary involvement in Kilbourntown would reveal an aggregate of literally isolated people.

5

The Neighborhood

For the homemakers of Kilbourntown there seems little basis for doubting that the center of their world is the family. As Wilensky suggests, this is typical for urban America: "With striking consistency the recent studies of urban life underscore the nuclear family as the basic area of involvement for all types of urban populations. We find not a madly mobile, rootless mass, disintegrating for want of intimate ties, but an almost bucolic contentment with the narrow circle of kin and close friends, with the typical urbanite spending most of his leisure with the family at home, caring for the children, watching television, maintaining the home, reading. Occasionally he makes forays in the world outside, mainly to visit relatives, sometimes to demonstrate his highly held attachment to a formal organization or two."[1] There are, however, several things wrong with Wilensky's analysis. His stress on the nuclear rather than the extended family seems appropriate more for whites than blacks. Moreover, activities like television-watching and reading involve us in people and events outside the family; Wilensky seems to assume that any activity that takes place in the home increases familial involvement, but this is obviously wrong. Day-dreaming, for example, can alienate us from the family. On the whole, however, Wilensky's description can be accepted. The urban world is populated not by isolated individuals but by isolated families.

The point of this chapter and the next is to explore the nature of involvement outside the family. In this chapter we concentrate on the neighborhood, and especially the religious life of our respondents. The next chapter concerns the nation. In Chapter Three it was suggested that there were four foci of involvement in Kilbourntown: the self, the family, religion, and country. In this and the next chapter the last two of these foci will be discussed.

NEIGHBORHOOD INVOLVEMENT

City life can be defined in terms of the amount of "public activity". as Bahrdt calls it, that takes place among an aggregate of human beings. Behavior is public "where there is no all-inclusive unbroken network of intervening and negotiating connections, and where people meet constantly, enter into communication and stand in relationships to each other without the one being classified in a common social order for the other."[2] The city is the place of fleeting relationships and of individually negotiated relationships. The key to city life for Bahrdt is the absence of a "common social order" among people who interact with each other. The point is not that man is isolated, in a strict sense, but that the relations that do exist in a city are not part of some larger social structure of obligations and privileges.

What, then, is meant by a "common order"? To the exent that an aggregate of people have a set of shared beliefs about their mutual rights and responsibilities, which beliefs are conscious and relatively stable, there exists a "common order."

With some justification Wilensky has been critical of those who portray the urban man as cut off from human relationships: "Whatever the mobility of the population, intimate contacts with relatives, neighbors, and friends are a universal feature of urban life at home in the local community. ...Such contacts are also a universal feature of life at work. Even in the huge workplace where many thousands mass for the daily routine, the informal workgroup seems destined to go on performing its usual functions of controlling the workplace: initiating new members, deciding how far to go along with the boss, and making work a bit more like play. There is no evidence that human relations are any more atomized at work than in the local community and neighborhood...."[3]

Granted. Urban life does not mean isolation or atomization. But, it does mean a profound change in the nature of social relations. In the city the relationships we have are not unified or tied together; they are not part of a common structure. Rather they are experienced as discrete events. Social life lacks unity.

But does an absence of unity in our social relationships mean a sense of alienation? A man may be deeply involved in a tennis match, then deeply involved with a woman, then thoroughly immersed in a Hemingway novel, then deeply preoccupied with his job of teaching, then engrossed in the daily newspaper on the subway ride home. Is he alienated? Over time the answer must be "yes." His life lacks a unity, lacks a sense of oneness over time. Will he feel alienated? We do not know. It has already been pointed out that we do not know the relation between alienation and a person's time perspective. Perhaps some people are influenced only by immediate events, others by weekly events, and others by the degree of unity among the high points in their entire life.

It seems clear, however, that the absence of a social order uniting our various relations is at least a potential source of alienation. The question we pose in this chapter is whether there is any social order unifying the residents of Kilbourntown. These neighbors will interact with each other. Is it likely that these neighborhood relations will be experienced as part of some common social structure?

The state, of all organizations, does give a status to nearly everyone in K-3; at least most of the adults must be citizens. This source of social order will be discussed in the next chapter. In this chapter we are interested in what have been called intermediate institutions, i.e., organizations other than the family or the state. The word "intermediate" is poor because it suggests that an organization is subordinate to the state. But can this be said, for instance, of religious organizations? Can one say that the Catholic churches in Kilbourntown are subordinate to the state? The answer must be "yes" and "no". We are interested in sources of a "common order" that are not part of the state. We shall refer to these simply as nonpolitical orders.

The question we seek to answer in this chapter, then, is as follows: To what degree are the residents of Kilbourntown unified by nonpolitical sources of order? Strictly speaking, each individual has his own personal neighborhood, i.e., his own set of spatially based relationships. But we have not determined the personal neighborhood of each of our 623 housemakers. Rather, we have simply assumed that many of these spatial relationships will involve their fellow Kilbourntown housewives, and we have investigated the extent to which each of our respondents shares a "common order" with the other respondents.

TYPES OF NONPOLITICAL ORDERS

Many community studies, and especially those interested in political power, focus not on involvement but integration. The behavior of human beings may be efficiently coordinated without these people experiencing any sense of involvement with each other. The coordination may be so far removed as to be invisible. For example, workers belonging to two companies owned by the same corporation may be coordinated by that corporation without the workers in one company feeling involved with those in the other company. Similarly, coalitions of political bosses and business leaders may coordinate people without these people being aware that their lives are interrelated. Our concern is not integration but involvement.

Moreover, we are not interested in how the people of Kilbourntown are related to those living elsewhere. Our focus is on the neighborhood, on what Warren has called the "horizontal pattern."[4]

What types of nonpolitical orders exist in Kilbourntown?

The classic study of neighborhood order is the work of William F. Whyte. Not only did he find that "common orders" did exist, but he reported that, for many of the young males he studied, neighborhood structures were more important than the household.

> Home plays a very small role in the group activites of the corner boy. Except when he eats, sleeps, or is sick, he is rarely at home, and his friends always go to his corner first when they want to find him. Even the corner boy's name indicates the dominant importance of the gang in his activities. It is possible to associate with a group of men for months and never discover the family names of more than a few of them. Most are known by nicknames attached to them by the group. Furthermore, it is easy to overlook the distinction between married and single men. The married man regularly sets aside one evening a week to take out his wife. There are other occasions when they go out together and entertain together, and some corner boys devote more attention to their wives than others, but married or single, the corner boy can be found on his corner almost every night of the week.[5]

Whyte's study was done in an Italian district of Boston before World War II. Such male groups as the corner boys he describes, may, however, exist in Kilbourntown. But, more generally, Whyte's work points to the possible importance of informal groups. By informal it is meant not only that the rules regarding rights and responsibilities are not written down, but that the group is not visible to the general public. It is not open to all; rather it usually exists for a small number of people and does not seek publicity beyond that small aggregate. Basically, informal means nonpublic—not open to the public, not known by the public, not recognized by the public. For their members informal groups provide a common order.

A second form of a "common order" is a formal organization. We shall discuss three types: work organizations, voluntary associations and religious organizations. The last is sometimes considered a voluntary association. But the sense of compulsion many people feel to attend a church makes it difficult to consider church membership as voluntary. Similarly, since many people must work, it is customary to differentiate work organizations from voluntary associations.

The third and last form of a "common order" we call the advice-structures. By this we refer to the various professional individuals[6] and agencies available in our society to people seeking help with their problems; the concept refers to most welfare institutions, but it is broader than this category since it also includes psychiatrists and private charity organizations; moreover, it also refers to doctors, priests, and so on to the extent that they are sources of help to people in ways not related to their professional, special qualification; so, if people consult their doctor about family problems, which are outside his speciality, the doctor is part of an advice-structure. In general, advice-structures include all those professionals whose help is sought in solving what we today call "social problems."

Advice-structures fulfill what Warren has called the "mutual support function." This refers "to the type of help which is proffered in those instances where individual and family crises present needs which are not otherwise satisfied in the usual pattern of organized social behavior. Examples are illness, economic need, and problems of family functioning."[7]

To what extent do advice-structures provide "common order"? It is clear that common membership in an informal or formal organization provides a common understanding about responsibilities and rights among the members. A similar understanding exists between advisors and clients, although it may not be too clear to the clients what their rights are. But the idea of an order governing the advisor-client relation does exist in any advice-structure. On the other hand, while members of an organization are conscious of an order governing the relations among them, clients even of the same advisor are not aware of such an order. Advice-structures bind people vertically but not horizontally.

Of course, the amount of order given to a person's life by membership in an organization will vary considerably. To be a member of a religious sect could mean that all of one's life is oriented to a set of religious norms. Moreover, the sect members may live near each other and be each other's constant companions. These sect members would experience life as a meaningful whole; their religious organization would have provided them with an order that tied together all daily events. On the other hand a person might be a member of the local historical society. Compared to a sect it would order little of the person's life. Members of the historical society would find it difficult to relate most of what they did in life to the rules of the historical society. Organizations differ quite markedly, therefore, in the degree to which they provide a non-political order, but all organizations and advice-structures do provide some order.

To what extent do these sources of order exist in Kilbourntown?

INFORMAL ORGANIZATIONS

We attempted to find out if there are sociometric stars in Kilbourntown, i.e., individuals around whom our respondents cluster and through whom they are interrelated. This section is based on all 748 respondents, i.e., it includes everyone we interviewed. It became clear to us that we had found little informal organization in K-3 among our respondents, and that obviously this conclusion was also valid for our subsample of 623 female homemakers.

We used three questions to find informal leaders: the "think about" question and our inquiries about from whom the respondents seek advice on family problems and on money problems. It is true that strictly speaking the absence of leaders does not mean the absence of informal groups. However, informal organizations often lack an elaborate structure and thus are especially dependent on the relations of followers to leaders. Whyte's study of Cornerville clearly portrays the nonofficial structure as a network of personal loyalties centering on a few key leaders. We assume that without the charisma of leaders informal groupings tend to come and go and are of little significance. Our analysis of informal structure, then, concentrates on evidence concerning the existence of common allegiance to informal leaders.

On the 748 questionnaires collected, thirty-four names appeared two or more times in response to the "think about" question. Six people received more than two mentions: Presidents Kennedy and Johnson each appeared five times, God is mentioned seven times, two Protestant ministers each received three mentions, and one person unknown to us appeared three times; twenty-eight other individuals were mentioned twice. Two points are clear: 1) The most frequently mentioned are nonlocals (presidents and God); the charisma that does exist for our respondents directs their interest either to spiritual beings or to national events; and 2) There is little informal local structure among our respondents; at most 9 percent of our total sample of 748 shared a local "leader" with at least one other person, i.e., 9 percent of the sample think about at least one person who is also thought about by another person in our sample[8]. It must be clear that this 9 percent do not share a common "leader;" rather this 9 percent is composed of clusters of two to three people who mentioned the same name. The "think about" question did not reveal any local charismatic figures.

We, also, considered the specific persons mentioned in response to the two advice questions. The total sample of 748 respondents mentioned a total of 286 people from whom they seek advice. No one was mentioned more than twice, and only three names appear twice: God, a pastor, and someone else whose status is unknown to us. This total of 286 includes professional people who will be discussed in the next section.

Quite clearly there appear to be no local leaders around whom neighborhood structures could form. This does not mean that informal organizations do not exist. For instance, it is possible that some Kilbourntown homemakers get together regularly for gossip and coffee. But such contacts themselves do not produce a "common order." Simply because people regularly get together does not mean that a stable and conscious set of mutual rights and responsibilities have developed. It should be noted that our inquiry about voluntary associations included a specific question about "social clubs;" these will be discussed later.

ADVICE-STRUCTURES

Advice-structures include all the people who seek advice about their problems from professional people as well as all the professionals consulted. As already indicated only three specific people were mentioned more than once. No professionals dominate advice-giving in K-3.[9] In this section we want to discuss the significance of advice-structures as well as their nature.

Table 5-1 presents data on the type of people from whom our respondents seek advice. (For the remainder of this chapter the analysis is based on the sample of 623 homemakers.) A total of thirty-one persons seek advice on family problems from professional people; forty-five respondents seek advice on money problems from professionals. Considering both types of problems

TABLE 5-1

TYPES OF PEOPLE FROM WHOM RESPONDENTS SEEK ADVICE ON
MONEY OR FAMILY PROBLEMS[1]

Advice on money	Advice on family						
	Minister or priest	Social worker	Misc. public service	Doctor	Personal relation	No help sought	Total (45)
Minister or priest	1				1	2	4
Social worker					2	5	7
Employer						4	4
Credit union			1			4	5
Loan company or bank	1				2	9	12
Landlord						2	2
Misc. public service	1					3	4
Doctor	1						1
Attorney					1	5	6
Personal relation	5					46	52
No help sought	14	2	4	1	42	475	
	—	–	–	–	—	—	—
Total (31)	23	2	5	1			

1. To find out how many people seek advice from any one type read down to the "total" row for family problems and across to the "total" column for money problems. "Personal relation" means advice is sought from a nonprofessional. The body of the table shows the combinations of help activities for the two problems, so the "1" in the first column in the upper left corner of the table means that one person seeks advice on both problems from a minister or priest.

a total of seventy-one respondents (11 percent of the homemakers) seek help from professionals.

It is interesting to note the types of professionals influential in Kilbourntown. The last column on the right of Table 5-1 contains the totals for the various categories used in the table with regard to seeking advice on money problems. Understandably, loan companies and banks have the highest frequency. They are composed of professionals trained to solve monetary problems and they are used. The situation is quite different regarding family problems. People with such problems make significant use of only one source of help, religious specialists. This dependence on the religious institutions reflects both a traditional closeness between religion and family and the relative absence of appropriately trained specialists. Industrial society has trained many people to handle its money problems, but few to care for personal problems. The absence of the latter type of specialist is especially flagrant in the ghettos.

One result of this is the significance of the religious institution in Kilbourntown, though use of ministers and priests as sources of advice is not limited to K-3. In a study of the Hough ghetto in Cleveland, respondents were asked to indicate from a list which sources they would utilize for help in times of personal trouble: "For help with personal problems three sources of help accounted for 76.6 percent of the first choices: clergyman first, relatives second, and lawyers or doctors third. Social agencies were mentioned as first choices by only 6.5 per cent of the respondents...."[10] Our results suggest that in fact people seek advice more frequently from relatives than professionals. But the study in Hough and ours in Kilbourntown document the importance of the religious institution in the lives of the residents of these northern ghettos. Matthews and Prothro came to the same conclusion in their study of southern politics; one-third of all leaders mentioned by black people were preachers: "No other single occupational group receives anything close to the number of leadership nominations given to preachers."[11]

The counterpart to the importance of the religious organizations is the insignificance of the "social workers" (this was the way our respondents described the advisors in question). About one out of every six respondents live on welfare. The insignificant part played by social workers in the advice-structure strongly suggests the colossal failure of the welfare program to win the confidence of the people they help.

It must be remembered that the advice questions asked about the person our respondents "most often" go to for advice. These questions did not gather information on the occasional use of professionals.

FORMAL ORGANIZATION

WORK ORGANIZATION   Data were collected on the occupation of the bread-winner. We asked about the kind of company that the breadwinner worked for at the time of the interview or, if the person was unemployed, during the last period of employment. Even though everyone did not report a specific employer, for all 748 respondents a list of 288 companies was accumulated. No further analysis was performed, since it is obvious that employment is quite dispersed. Employment of breadwinners in the same work organizations could offer a "common order" based on relations at work. But the dispersion of employment prevents such a nonpolitical order being significant in Kilbourntown.

There are, of course, community-level organizations whose purpose is to coordinate individual companies. If these coordinating agencies were effective in unifying the companies, then these agencies could provide some order even for people who work for different employers. But as Warren has said: "It is interesting to note that even where the horizontal relationship among business enterprises is formalized in such an organization [as the chamber of commerce], the ties of one local business enterprise to another within that organization are much weaker and much more peripheral than are the vertical ties of the respective branch business enterprises to their own particular national companies." "Though organizations like the chamber of commerce afford a means of horizontal integration at the community level, they characteristically coordinate these organizations only superficially."[12]

RELIGIOUS ORGANIZATIONS

Several times in our work we have noted the importance of ministers or priests in the lives of our respondents: such people seem to be the most significant local, nonfamilial sources of influence for our homemakers. The question arises, therefore, to what extent do religious organizations unify K-3? By religious organizations in this section we mean specific churches or parishes.

As with work organizations the respondents are dispersed over a wide range of religious organizations; we reviewed the specific titles of churches mentioned by our respondents and tried to eliminate any error due to different persons using slightly different titles in referring to the same churches. Whenever we believed different titles referred to the same church we pooled the respondents associated with each title. We also eliminated those individuals who gave generic references such as "Methodist" or "Congregationalist"; we still ended up with a list of 112 different churches.

The vast majority of churches (96 out of 112) attended by our respondents have five or less of the respondents as members. Table 5-2 shows the distribu-

TABLE 5–2

DISTRIBUTION OF CHURCHES RESPONDENTS BELONG TO

(By number of respondent-members[1])

Respondent-members	Number of churches
1–5	96
6–10	8
11–15	4
16–20	0
21–25	2
26–30	1
31–35	1
	112

1. For this analysis we used only the whites and blacks in our sample, N=578; of these, 415 named a specific church to which they go.

tion of churches by the number of respondent-members. The single church with the largest number of respondents as members is a Roman Catholic church; thirty-four respondents belong to it. The use of a territorial basis for defining church boundaries gives the Roman Catholic Church an edge in being able to unify neighborhoods. However, the majority of the respondents belong to churches which have few, i.e., ten or less, respondents as members.

This dispersion of church membership is matched by a dispersion of

TABLE 5–3

DISTRIBUTION OF RESPONDENTS

(By type of church they attend and by color of respondent)

Type of church	White(N=169)	Black(N=409)
Attend nonintegrated church[1]	30%	47%
Attend integrated church	39	20
Did not name specific church[2]	10	14
Do not attend church	15	11
No response noted	7	9[3]

1. "Nonintegrated" means that in our sample we found people of only one color attending these churches. Only whites and blacks were considered.

2. These people usually responded: "Baptist," "Methodist," and so on.

3. This total includes nine who gave only a general location and two who gave a minister's name that we were unable to assign to a specific church.

church location. We could locate only 19 of the 112 churches mentioned by our respondents in K-3 or within two blocks of its boundaries. Religious devotion scatters the respondents over a large area of the city.

Dispersion weakens the ability of churches to give order to life in Kilbourntown. This weakness is increased by the fact that church membership fails to significantly cut across racial lines. The whites belong to forty-four churches; the blacks belong to eighty churches. Whites and blacks share only twelve churches. Table 5-3 shows the distribution of respondents according to whether or not they attend integrated churches; "integrated" means that both whites and blacks from our sample attend the church. (Using only our sample to determine whether or not a church is integrated means that we have underestimated the number of integrated churches.) Table 5-3 gives a rather positive picture for whites; 39 percent attend integrated churches. But the picture changes when we look at details. There are only six integrated churches that have at least five respondents as members. The ratios of minority-majority (depending upon the specific church, the minority might be white or black) in the six integrated churches are - 1:6, 1:7.5, 1:10, 1:10.5, 1:12, and 1:25. These ratios take into consideration only the homemakers who participated in our study. The ratio of whites to blacks in our sample is 1:2.4; the church with the closest ratio (1:6) has only seven respondents as members, and these are mostly white, which is the reverse of the K-3 neighborhood as a whole. It would be more appropriate to write this church's ratio as 6:1, which is quite different from the white-black ratio of 1:2.4 for our sample. In all, forty-one respondents, thirty-six whites and five blacks, are members of integrated churches with a ratio of 10:1 or less (and with at least six respondents as members). It appears, therefore, that the majority of our respondents do not attend integrated churches, and that the percentage of whites in integrated churches is misleading, because these whites seem to attend churches that have only a very small black membership.[13]

Warren had noted the significance of religious organizations in American life: "more Americans are members of churches than any other type of voluntary association. ..." At the same time he recognized the importance of segmentation: "On the basis of membership and participation in one church rather than another, community people are separated from each other in an important aspect of their social participation, as they participate in one or another of the 259 religious denominations having churches in American communities."[14] It should be remembered that our figure of 112 churches refers to specific churches or parishes and not to denominations. Many of these churches are "store-front churches" belonging to no denomination. As Pinkney has noted—"The black community is noted for the number of churches it includes. Drake and Clayton enumerated some 500 churches in Chicago that served some 200,000 members. These churches represented more than 30 denomina-

TABLE 5–4

DISTRIBUTION OF CHURCH MEMBERSHIP

(By color of respondent)

Type of church	White (N=169)	Black (N=409)
Roman Catholic	37%	9%
Protestant churches	30	57
Episcopalian	(0)[1]	(.3)
Lutheran	(18)	(2)
Presbyterian	(.6)	(.6)
Congregationalist	(1)	(0)
Methodist	(5)	(5)
Baptist	(5)	(44)
Church of God in Christ	(.6)	(6)
Protestant sects	5	10
Miscellaneous	7	8
No church membership	21	17

1. In parentheses are the percentages belonging to specific Protestant churches.

tions. Seventy-five percent of these churches were store-front churches or 'house churches' with an average membership of fewer than 25 persons. A study of central Harlem in the 1960's enumerated 418 church buildings. Of this number only 122 were housed in conventional church buildings; 232 were located either in store fronts or in residential buildings; and the remainder were located in large meeting halls, private homes, or social agencies."[15] In black ghettos, generally, religious devotion scatters involvement among a large number of specific organizations. Through these organizations people interact and develop relationships with only a few neighbors. Religion can be only a weak source for a "common order" that would structure relationships among the residents of Kilbourntown.

DENOMINATIONS   By discussing only specific churches or parishes we exaggerate the amount of religious diversification. Structurally some churches are more closely linked than others. Table 5-4 shows the distribution of church membership by denomination. Among the whites 37 percent are Roman Catholic and 18 percent are Lutheran. Especially for the Catholics, the centralized religious structure suggests that there would be some meaningful coordination of the behavior of Catholics in our sample. But even if there is this coordination, will common membership in the same denomination produce an aggregate of people who know each other as members and who interact with each other in terms of a shared set of rules concerning mutual rights and responsibilities? This is not likely. Religious life is almost totally organized around the local, specific church or parish. There are, for instance, few common services. People of different Catholic parishes probably do not know each other. Catholics from different parishes remain "familiar strangers" to each other. The significance of the fact that 37 percent of the K-3 whites are Catholics lies in the potential suggested by this percentage. Both the Catholic and Lutheran churches in Kilbourntown, and in Milwaukee generally, are numerically significant churches that could do much to create a sense of a "common order." But this potential will be underutilized as long as these denominations put so much stress on individual churches.

But is it even a good policy to suggest that churches try to provide a "common order?" As the data in Table 5-4 suggest any attempt by one of the religious denominations to use membership in the denomination as a source of neighborhood structure would only unify a minority of respondents and would divide the population along racial lines. While 37 percent of the whites are Catholic, only 9 percent of the blacks are; while 44 percent of the blacks are Baptist, only 5 percent of the whites are. The religious pluralism of the United States, exemplified in Table 5-4, makes it difficult for a single denomination to serve as a neighborhood source of a "common order."

Moreover, the types of religious organization prevalent in the United States pose a special problem from the viewpoint of community-building. Despite the rise of ecumenicalism, belonging to one branch of Christianity usually implies a rejection of all other religious groups. A person can be a member of the P.T.A. without being against anyone. This is not true of most religious groups, where membership implies rejection of the denomination not joined. Such groups polarize a community, and so we call them "polarizing organizations." Since most Christian groups are polarizing organizations, their very existence creates conflict, i.e., negative involvement.

There are interdenominational organizations in Milwaukee—The Interdenominational Ministerial Alliance, The Milwaukee Associates in Urban Ministries, and The Greater Milwaukee Council of Churches. The very fact there are three such organizations suggests that the same proliferation of religious organizations is now taking place on the supradenominational level. Moreover, we doubt if the vast majority of people in K-3 are aware that these organizations exist. More important perhaps, these interdenominational organizations do not include as members many of the churches attended by Kilbourntown residents. For instance, the Lutheran and Catholic churches have not been allowed at the time of this study to join the Council of Churches. We tried to check how many of the churches attended by our black respondents belong to these organizations. The task was made difficult by our not knowing the names of all the pastors. It is our impression, however, that many of the sect-type and small Baptist churches are not associated with any of these supradenominational organizations. In all, we are sure that fourteen churches, with about one-third of our black churchgoers as members, are associated with at least one interdenominational organization. Approaching the problem somewhat differently, we found nineteen churches within K-3 or within two blocks of its boundaries; ten are not members of any interfaith organization; seven churches, six of which are Baptist, are members of the Interdenominational Ministerial Alliance. The evidence suggests that a significant number of our respondents do not belong to a church that is a member of any supradenominational organization. Because of this, and because there is a proliferation of interfaith organizations, and because about a fifth of our sample report no church membership, it is doubtful if any supradenominational religious organization could serve as a source of a "common order" in a neighborhood like Kilbourntown.

Moreover, Warren's judgement must be kept in mind, that "the local councils of churches are admittedly and deliberately weak in the sense that they do not seek organizational unification.... By no means does it approach in systemic importance the tie which most churches have to their extracommunity denominational bodies."[16] Interdenominational organizations are too weak to be significant in the life of the average person.

TABLE 5–5

DISTRIBUTION OF ORGANIZATIONAL MEMBERSHIPS

(By color of respondent)				
	Number of memberships			
Type of organization	White(169)		Black(408)	
Church	134	(79%)[1]	341	(83%)[1]
P.T.A.	12	(7%)	76	(19%)
Union	11	(7%)	27	(7%)
Civil rights organization	1[2]		15[2]	
Other instrumental organizations	10[3]		6[3]	
Social clubs	23[2]		29[2]	

1. This is the percent of our sample who said they attend a church. There are some cases in which the interviewer did not record a response; these are counted as "no church membership" cases. Also five black respondents did not know the name of the church they attend, and these are treated as "no church membership" cases.

2. We cannot calculate the percent of subsample, because the same individual might belong to two or three organizations.

3. Examples of such organizations are: the Democratic Party, the Lutheran Association, and the County Historical Society.

SOLIDARITY IN A SLUM

VOLUNTARY ASSOCIATION

We asked the respondents if they are members of any fraternal organizations like lodges or auxiliaries, social clubs, veterans' organizations, community improvement groups, labor unions, civil rights groups, P.T.A. (or Home and School), political organizations, church-related groups, or any other groups.

As with church membership, there is little concentration of attachment within the array of available voluntary associations. The white and black respondents belong to a total of sixty-five organizations, seven of which have members from both races. Once again, not only is membership disbursed but it divides the neighborhood along racial lines.

Our analysis does not include memberships in church-related organizations. Such memberships are especially frequent among the blacks, but since we have already discussed the significance of religious associations, church-related voluntary associations are excluded from the present analysis.[17] The importance of these organizations, however, should not be overlooked. Babchuk and Booth found in a study of the residents of Nebraska that over a four year period 45 percent of their sample had belonged at least for a while to a church-related voluntary association.[18] This underlines the importance of religious institutions in the life of Americans, an importance often overlooked by those who discuss the "mass society."

Table 5-5 summarizes the data on organization membership; information on church affiliation is included for purposes of comparison. Perhaps the most striking feature of associational life in Kilbourntown, leaving aside the churches, is that it is minimally voluntary. Eighty-eight respondents are members of the Parent-Teacher's Association; this probably refers to several different local branches of the P.T.A., but we did not collect data describing which branch members belonged to. Thirty-eight respondents are union-members; these memberships, however, are spread out over sixteen different unions. The P.T.A. and the unions are significant in Kilbourntown, but it is noteworthy that both types of organizations are minimally voluntary. If you are a parent with a child in school, pressure is applied either by the P.T.A. or the school or both to join the P.T.A. Similarly, many workers either have to join a union to get a job or are pressured into joining a union by their fellow workers. There is very little truly voluntary participation in formal organizations among the Kilbourntown residents.

The P.T.A. and the unions do offer some basis for unity. However, about 40 percent of the members of these organizations reported attending meetings only rarely. Whether this is because meetings are rare or because our respondents are not interested, we can not determine. But whatever the reason the rare attendance lessens the significance of these organizations. The P.T.A. does stand out, however, as the most significant voluntary organization in Kilbourntown. Given this fact, it is regretable that this organization plays such an insignificant role in neighborhood life. It is true, however, that since our data were collected at least a few branches of the P.T.A. in Milwaukee showed signs of taking some initiative in the formulation of educational policy. For the most part, at least in Milwaukee, the P.T.A. is a tool of the school board and the school principals. Given this passivity, membership in the P.T.A. cannot mean much to people. But the potential of the P.T.A. must not be overlooked. It does reach into many homes, and it does relate to something that is an important part of life, i.e., education. An active P.T.A. could give residents of a neighborhood a sense of common purpose and shared responsibility. An active P.T.A. could give a sense of a "common order;" it could turn "familiar strangers" into fellow committee-members or at least fellow campaigners in a good and serious cause.

The same potential resides in civil rights groups, but as can be seen in Table 5-5, only one white respondent and fifteen black respondents are members of such groups. The only organization of some numerical significance is the NAACP. It has twelve members, all black; CORE has two members, the Urban League one member; a local civil rights group has one member. All other types of voluntary organizations account for sixty-eight memberships spread among at least forty-four associations.

As Table 5-5 clearly indicates, religious organizations dominate non-household, neighborhood life in Kilbourntown.[19]

PARTICIPATION IN RELIGIOUS RITUAL

Each respondent was asked: "Do you go to church?" If the answer was "yes", the interviewee was asked whether she attended meetings "frequently, occasionally, or rarely?". These categories were used, because they allowed us to use the same predetermined responses for a variety of organizations. The church-question was part of a battery of questions about different kinds of voluntary associations. To minimize confusion we decided to use the same set of responses for each organization, and since meeting-frequencies varied from one organization to another, we could not use specific responses like weekly, monthly, and the like. Answering "monthly" for church-attendance, which is possible at least weekly, would not reflect the same involvement as attending a political club "monthly", if this organization meets only once a month. Therefore, the more subjective categories such as "frequently" were used. In this way it was hoped that the individual would alter her frame of reference for each organization, i.e., if she attended just about all the meetings, no matter how often they occurred, she would say "frequently." This is a bit idealistic. The categories used are vague, and ambiguity cannot be avoided; the middle category "occasionally" was probably especially difficult to use. However, given the limitations imposed by all the objectives we were trying to accomplish, rather subjective categories seemed to be the best set of responses available.

In retrospect it is clear we took the wrong approach. Considering only the church-attendance question, 72 out of 341 black church members do not have a frequency-response recorded for them. We are not sure why this is so, but we strongly suspect that our respondents answered in more concrete terms like "weekly" or "twice a week," and that our amateur interviewers did not know how to handle the situation. Of course we should have anticipated this problem or noticed it during the course of the study. In any case the abstract categories used appear to have been quite inappropriate for our church-attendance question. On the other hand, our respondents did not seem to have the same difficulty for all types of organizations. While roughly one out of five church members have no attendance recorded, this was true for only one social club member out of thirty-nine. We suspect that the categories seemed more inappropriate, the more regularly and frequently an organization met. And since churches meet regularly and frequently, we ended up with a large number of unusable cases; 29 white and 75 black cases were lost, because no frequency-response was recorded.

From the point of view of neighborhood involvement, church attendance is important not only because of the large number of respondents who belong to churches. Equally important is the fact that religious ritual is oriented toward solidarity-building. This is more true of the more formal churches like Catholicism and of the sects than of the sermon-oriented Protestant churches like the Congregationalist. But most of our respondents belong to the more emotion-arousing denominations like the Baptists and the Methodists, as well as to the sects and more formalized churches. The religious services our respondents attend are among mankind's most successful attempts to develop occasions for making someone feel involved with others. It is true that often today these rituals are failures. For instance, many Catholics are more annoyed than pleased at church services. But among the myriad occasions offered to man, even contemporary man, the church service remains an outstanding example of an involvement-enhancing situation.[20]

AGE, COLOR AND CHURCH ATTENDANCE

Argyle reported that once past thirty years of age, people tend to go to church more often the older they get.[21] Our data are generally consistent with this proposition (see Table 5-6). The highest percentages of nonattenders are among those seventeen to thirty-nine years of age, while frequent attendance occurs most frequently among those sixty or over. On the other hand, our data suggest that regarding attendance at religious rituals aging involves two dis-

TABLE 5–6

FREQUENCY OF CHURCH ATTENDANCE BY AGE AND COLOR OF RESPONDENT

	Color and frequency of church attendance									
Age	*White*					*Black*				
	Not a church attender[1]	*Rare*	*Occa-sional*	*Frequent*	*Sample size (N)*	*Not a church attender*	*Rare*	*Occa-sional*	*Frequent*	*Sample size (N)*
17–39	33%	7%	27%	33%	(30)	20%	11%	38%	32%	(213)
40–59	21	13	31	35	(48)	14	12	41	33	(81)
60 plus	25	12	12	51	(59)	13	6	22	59	(32)

1. This includes all respondents who definitely said they belong to no church as well as those cases in which the interviewer simply did not record an answer to the church question.

unct processes: 1) As people move from youth to middle age, they cease to be outside religious institutions but do not necessarily go very frequently to church; thus, for both blacks and whites respondents over forty are more often church members than people below forty; and 2) As people move from the middle years to old age, they tend to go more frequently to church. Thus, there is a dramatic difference, for both whites and blacks, between those sixty and above and those below sixty in the percentage of frequent church-goers. The first process brings people into a church; the second makes them active members.

The idea of a two stage process as people age is consistent with the little we know about the motivation behind religious participation. As people produce a family, pressures are felt to join a church.[22] Young parents begin worrying about their children's upbringing and join a church to ensure that their children will be exposed to religion. Also, as people begin to age, it is probably more and more "expected" by family and friends that adults will attend a church. The move into the religious institution is often the result of external pressures, i.e., pressures that have nothing to do with truly personal, religious problems, so that it would be expected that such people would not be frequent church-goers. On the other hand, as people age and face death and possibly loneliness, they want to go to church; attendance is voluntary. When people reach old age, they must personally face the problems that religions are meant to solve, such as death. Frequent church attendance in old age, then, is understandable.

The differences by color are less significant than the differences by age. More whites, however, remain outside the religious institution.

MOBILITY AND CHURCH ATTENDANCE

Lee used the number of local friends and the number of organizations joined as criteria of involvement. He summarized his data on mobility and neighborhood involvement as follows: "It appears that newcomers to a locality become involved, up to a given low level, quite quickly. Thereafter, they remain more or less static for about five years. after which their involvement begins to increase steadily."[23] Lee's use of five years as a significant point of differentiation is interesting. Does his analysis apply to church attendance?

Table 5-7 presents the relevant data for blacks; there were too few whites for analysis.

Considering the "frequently" column, there is a clear pattern. Regardless of age, there is a slight tendency for this percentage to increase, the longer respondents have lived in Milwaukee.

But the data are not consistent for nonattenders. Comparing those who have lived fifteen years or less in Milwaukee with the rest, the relative newcomers are less often nonattenders among the young but more often nonattenders among the older respondents (i.e., those forty to fifty-nine years of age). The

TABLE 5–7

FREQUENCY OF CHURCH ATTENDANCE BY AGE OF RESPONDENT
AND YEARS LIVED IN MILWAUKEE

(For Blacks)

		Frequency of church attendance				
Age	Years lived in Milwaukee	Not a church attender	Rare	Occasional	Frequent	(N)
17–39	0–15[1]	19%	13%	38%	30%	(175)
	(0–5)[2]	(30)	(16)	(29)	(25)	(73)
	(6–10)	(14)	(12)	(43)	(31)	(51)
	(11–15)	(8)	(10)	(47)	(35)	(51)
	(16–35)		3	34	37	(38)
40–59	0–15	15	20	33	30	(40)
	16–50	10	3	50	36	(40)
60 and over	(Insufficient cases for analysis)					(32)
						(325)[3]

1. We had sufficient cases to make further breakdowns on length of residence only among these young, mobile people.

2. The respondents seventeen to thirty-nine years old who have lived in Milwaukee fifteen years or less are further broken down into those who have lived in Milwaukee five years or less, six to ten years, and eleven to fifteen years. In parentheses are the percentages for these subcategories.

3. Seven respondents did not report age; one did not report length of residence in Milwaukee.

TABLE 5–8

FREQUENCY OF CHURCH ATTENDANCE BY YEARS LIVED IN MILWAUKEE

(For Blacks seventeen to thirty-nine years of age)

Years lived in Milwaukee	Frequency of church attendance		
	Rarely or not at all	*Occasional or frequent*	*Sample size (N)*
0–5	48%	54%	(73)
6–10	26	74	(51)
11–15	18	82	(51)
16–35	29	71	(38)

analysis is further complicated by the fact that among those seventeen to thirty-nine years of age the more detailed breakdown on years in Milwaukee suggests a curvilinear relation between years in Milwaukee and percentage of nonattenders. The percentages are: 30 percent (zero to five years in Milwaukee), 14 percent, (six to ten years), 8 percent (eleven to fifteen years), and 26 percent (sixteen or more years). Since there were too few cases to perform more detailed analyses on those over thirty-nine years of age, we will restrict our further comments on mobility to the data on the young respondents.

To get a clearer picture of what might be happening, we collapsed the church-attendance categories as shown in Table 5-8. It seems clear that, at least for our young people, newcomers attend church less often than the rest of the respondents reported in the table. The dominant fact suggested by Table 5-8 is that newcomers tend to remain outside the churches. Consistent with Lee's analysis, there does seem to be an initial period of about five years when newcomers less actively participate in religious rituals.[24]

HOUSEHOLD FAMILY SIZE AND CHURCH ATTENDANCE

The size of the household could be important in several ways: 1) Isolated people might more often go to church seeking companionship; 2) People with large households might be too busy to go to church very often; or 3) People with children might go to church often out of a sense of duty to their children. Table 5-9 presents the relevant data for black people only; there are too few white cases for analysis.

Among the young those with very large families (9 plus) clearly go to church often. The idea that some women may be too busy at home to go to church seems completely without foundation. The fact that all other household sizes are roughly the same in church attendence suggests that household size itself is not important. It seems probable that religious people are likely to be ones who have very large households both because charity dictates that they help needy relatives and because of the high value often placed on children by Christian ministers and priests. Clearly there is no evidence among the young that household chores are a significant influence on church attendance.

Among the older black respondents there seems to be a curvilinear relation. But two warnings are necessary: 1) The subsample sizes are small, and 2) The "6 plus" category contains two size-categories ("6-8" and "9 plus") that appear to be quite distinct among the young; because of sample-size problems we had to collapse these two categories. The only tentative conclusion that seems worth making is that possibly isolates do go to church less often then other people. It may be that the reason for the increase in the percentage of people who attend church rarely or never among those respondents living in households of six or more people is that household chores may affect older people more than younger ones; it is possible that middle-aged people begin to lose interest in life so that their plans are more easily affected by inconveniences.

To check further on the significance of isolation we investigated the

TABLE 5-9

FREQUENCY OF CHURCH ATTENDANCE: BY AGE OF RESPONDENT
AND HOUSEHOLD FAMILY SIZE

		(For blacks)		
		Frequency of church attendance		
Age[1]	Household family size	Rarely or not at all	Occasional or frequent	Sample size (N)
17–39	1	(Too few cases)		(4)
	2	40%	60%	(30)
	3–5	33	67	(84)
	6–8	33	67	(61)
	9 plus	15	85	(32)
40–59	1	33	67	(18)
	2	18	82	(22)
	3–5	21	79	(24)
	6 plus[2]	33	67	(15)

1. There are too few cases of black respondents sixty and over to analyze.

2. Note that the categories "6–8" and "9 plus" are combined.

TABLE 5–10

FREQUENCY OF CHURCH ATTENDANCE: BY HOUSEHOLD
FAMILY SIZE

(Among white respondents aged sixty and above)

| Household family size | *Frequency of church attendance* | | |
	Attends rarely or not at all	*Occasional or frequent*	*Sample size (N)*
1	48%	52%	(25)
2 plus	23	77	(31)

relation between isolation and church attendance among the white respondents aged sixty and above (see Table 5-10); this is the only age range among the whites in which there are sufficient cases for analysis. As can be seen, the isolated women attend church less often. It could be that isolated elderly women are older than the nonisolated elderly and attend church less often because they more frequently suffer from physical handicaps. But even very elderly women should be able to attend church occasionally if they really want to.

Two types of people stand out in the analysis of household size; 1) Young people with large households often go to church; and 2) Isolates tend not to be frequent church-attenders.

CONCLUSION

Sociologically speaking, the city means the dominance of public activity, and, therefore, of fleeting and individually negotiated relationships. The city is the failure to experience unity over time in one's relationships.

Kilbourntown deserves to be called part of a city. We found no truly significant source of nonpolitical order outside the family. The major characteristic of Kilbourntown neighborhood life is dispersion—there are no local, informal leaders or professional advisors around whom the sample clusters, and our respondents are associated with at least 288 employers, 112 specific churches, and 65 different voluntary associations.[25] This dispersion of social life beyond the family makes the emergence of a common neighborhood social order impossible.

Our respondents jostle against others in the stores, observe people around them going to church, watch parties gather at different houses, hear the car horns announcing new marriages, see the signs of death and sorrow, and continually pass children on the streets; our respondents are immersed in a crowd of people. At the same time that they are aware of these people, of their proximity, of their being part of the environment, still they cannot fit these people into any framework; these people remain isolated examples of people, a boy here, a screaming woman there.

Coleman has pointed out that neighborhood disorganization need not mean personal disorganization, which is true. The absence of neighborhood structure does not automatically produce mental illness. Coleman concludes: "Communities are becoming less and less the 'building blocks' of which society is composed. ... The new society emerging in the twentieth century may well have social organization without local community organization."[26] Similarly, Alexander has written that "this idea of recreating primary groups by artificial means is unrealistic and reactionary; it fails to recognize the truth about the open society. The open society is no longer centered around place-based groups; and the very slight acquaintances that do form round an artificial neighborhood are once again trivial; they are not based on genuine desire."[27] Both Coleman and Alexander see the neighborhood as doomed.

On the other hand, "The Open Group" (a group of British scholars) has recently suggested that "an attempt should now be made to base the foundations of local government on the communities to which people belong...." "Redrawing the map of local government to correspond with the maps that residents have inside their minds has obvious attractions. A system of neighborhood or urban parish councils would then be as much rooted in people's loyalties as any system could be...."[28]

In discussing the neighborhood it is important to keep distinct the ideas of intimacy and common order. A person cannot be intimate with an entire neighborhood, even if he chose to be. Neighborhood involvement can never be based on intimacy. As sources of neighborhood social order "The Open Group" has suggested local political councils; but surely religion and especially schools offer other opportunities for building neighborhood unity. For instance, if members of an area were responsible for the development of a wide range of educational facilities for themselves this would give some social meaning to the neighborhood and to neighborly relations.

But the major question is whether people themselves experience any desire for neighborhood unity. It seems evident to us that at least some people would feel alienated in neighborhoods like Kilbourntown because of the absence of unity or structure in their neighborhood social relations. The unrelatedness of social bonds would prevent some from experiencing life as a continuous oneness, as a continuous involvement. But how many people have this experience, and how great a source of alienation is it? When we know the answers to these questions, we will know the importance of neighborhood social orders.

But even though people may wish to structure their neighborhood, they are faced with a monstrous technical problem: In a world that requires integration on a massive scale, how can people produce involvement on the local level?

6

National Involvement
with George Gerharz

The residents of Kilbourntown do share one source of social order—the state[1]. Our research did not consider in detail the extent to which our respondents are involved in city or state politics. But the analyses of the "think about" and the "proud" questions presented in Chapter Three suggest that of all the political levels, the national seems to be the most significant. The nation is one of the four foci around which the lives of the respondents seem to revolve. In this chapter we are concerned with two questions: How involved are the respondents in the nation? What produces national involvement?

We must be clear, however, about the limitations of national involvement. Even if all the residents of Kilbourntown were deeply involved in the nation, this could not eliminate the source of alienation discussed in the last chapter. The modern state can not take the place of neighborhood structure. It is true that the nation provides all citizens with a set of goals and assigns to all of them rights and responsibilities, i.e., the nation does provide a common order. But for most citizens the relation of these goals, rights, and responsibilities to the daily routine of their lives is tenuous at best. It is nothing new to point out that citizenship usually means little to people beyond voting and paying taxes. The people in our daily life form an amorphous mass of "fellow citizens." Labelling each other as citizens influences our behavior but little.

On the other hand, the nation is not meaningless. It can give some unity to our lives and social meaning to our relationships. But it can do this only sporadically. The nation enters our lives at election times, during international crises, during demonstrations for social justice, and the like. The nation is neither meaningless nor a panacea for the cure of all alienation. The nation can not replace neighborhood structure, but it can give some unity to daily life.

THE MEASUREMENT OF NATIONAL INVOLVEMENT

National involvement means a sense of oneness with the nation. Our concept is similar to, but not identical with, the idea of nationalism. Weber noted that nationalism might be associated with such characteristics of a population as shared language, customs, or religion, or "memories of a common political destiny." But these conditions do not define nationalism; rather Weber referred to them as bases of nationalism. It is a sense of mission, a belief in the superiority of one's own cultural values and in the necessity of increasing the international prestige of these values that defines nationalism. Weber linked this condition to the struggle for prestige. Nationalism means that people are striving for a sense of personal value by championing their own culture. It finds expression in a missionary fervor to spread national values throughout the world.[2]

What is especially appealing about Weber's work is his separation of potential sources of nationalism from nationalism itself, a distinction that is similar to our differentiation of bases of involvement from the condition of involvement. However, national involvement is not the same as nationalism. The latter includes the former but goes beyond it. Nationalism requires that a person see himself united with a nation. But it means more. As Weber used it, nationalism also means a sense of superiority, so that people can feel justified in seeking the conversion of others to their own culture. Nationalism, therefore, means not only that people identify with the nation, but that they are proud of the culture associated with that nation, and furthermore, that they attempt to spread this culture over the face of the earth, because they believe it is superior to all other cultures.

Many discussions of nationalism lack the relative clarity of Weber's work. Boyd Shafer in his article "Toward a Definition of Nationalism" notes ten conditions often associated with the idea of nation: 1) a unit of territory, 2) cultural characteristics (including language), 3) sameness of social and economic institutions, 4) sovereign government, 5) belief in common history, 6) esteem for fellow nationals, 7) devotion to the nation and/or fellow nationals, 8) pride in the nation's achievements and sorrow in its tragedies, 9) hostility for groups threatening the nation, 10) hope for a glorious future and supremacy.[3] One or more of these elements is often used in defining nationalism. Generally, writers on this subject fail to distinguish: a) potential sources of national involvement (numbers 1 thru 5 above), b) measures of national involvement *per se* (none included in above list and none usually given), c) effects of national involvement (6-7 above) and d) nationalism (8-10 above).

In our own research we did not study nationalism but national involvement. Moreover, because of methodological problems we did not attempt to study a sense of oneness with the nation directly. Rather we studied whether or not a person showed the symptoms of national involvement. We tried to devise a measure of the extent to which a person acted as if he were involved with the nation.

Our questionnaire contained seven questions supposedly related to national involvement. Basically, these questions are: Would respondent feel ashamed if the American government admitted it was scared of Russian military power? Does the respondent feel proud when the United States is praised? Does respondent own an American flag? Does respondent get angry when she hears the United States criticized? Would respondent get angry if she saw a foreigner spit on the American flag? Does respondent believe a person who refuses to fight for his country should be expelled from the country? Does the respondent feel the war in Vietnam is not worth fighting? In our opinion too many attitude scales consist of repeating the same thought in different ways. To find that these items are interrelated only tells us that respondents are rational creatures, for the interrelations do not justify assuming the existence of an attitude independent of the test situation. Our approach was to choose seven items that appear quite different but that should be interrelated if our respondents are involved in the nation. In short, whether or not the seven items form a scale is a test to determine whether there is such a thing as a sense of oneness with the nation among our respondents. Our assumption was that if the seven items formed a scale, then a sense of national involvement really exists in Kilbourntown.

In what way are these seven questions related to national involvement? Our reasoning was as follows: a) People do not like to be criticized or admit they are scared, but they do like to be praised. Therefore, if they identify with the nation they will get angry if they hear people criticize the United States, will feel ashamed if American leaders say they are scared of Russia, but will feel proud if they hear the country praised; b) If people are involved with the nation, they will be more likely to own a flag, the symbol of the United States and they will be angry if they see someone spit on the flag; c) It is difficult for people to admit that what they are doing is wrong. Therefore, if they identify with their country, they will find it difficult to believe that people could be justified in criticizing a war in which their country is involved or that people could find a just reason for not fighting for their country. It was assumed that the seven topics covered by these assumptions would be interrelated only if there were such an attitude as national involvement.

When we considered the correlations among the seven items, it was clear that the flag ownership question was not a good one from our point of view. It is significantly related to only two of the six other questions. This is the most

TABLE 6–1

CORRELATIONS AMONG SIX QUESTIONS SUPPOSEDLY MEASURING
NATIONAL INVOLVEMENT FOR THE BLACK SUBSAMPLE (N=304)[1]

	Russian power	Praise U.S.	Criticise U.S.	Spit on flag	Refuse to fight	Vietnam war
1. Scared of russian power	—	.35	.34	N.S.[2]	N.S.[2]	.15[1]
2. Hear people praise U.S.	—	—	.42	.15	.22	.19
3. Hear people criticize U.S.	—	—	—	.25	.26	.15
4. People spit on flag	—	—	—	—	.20	.12
5. Refuse to fight for U.S.	—	—	—	—	—	.13
6. Vietnam war not worth fighting	—	—	—	—	—	—

1. Only those cases are used in which there was a usable response for the national involvement questions.

2. N.S. means the correlation was not statistically significant at the .05 level.

concrete of our questions, in which we asked the respondents whether or not they owned a flag; if they answered "no" we further inquired if they had ever thought about buying a flag. The absence of correlation with our other questions could mean that 1) owning a flag in the United States, and especially among poor people, is no indication of national involvement; flags are used so rarely that buying one just seems unimportant; or 2) the flag-ownership question, being concrete, is more revealing of national involvement than the other more attitudinal-type questions whose answers are less firmly grounded in facts and which, therefore, are more likely to reflect what the respondent thinks is a desirable response. We assumed that the first explanation was correct, but we could not rule out the second. Somewhat uneasily we simply eliminated the flag ownership question from our consideration.

Using only six questions, there were fifteen correlations only two of which were not statistically significant. The correlations for the black subsample are shown in Table 6-1. All the correlations are in the expected direction.

As the figures in Table 6-1 indicate the significant correlations are generally low. As would be expected, factor analysis revealed no single dominant factor; the first factor referred mainly to how proud respondents would be if they heard someone praise the U.S. (factor loading of .83) and how angry they would be if they heard someone criticize the U.S. (factor loading of .81). But this factor accounted for only 30 percent of the total variance. These two questions are the most "attitudinal" we have, i.e., they are very vague and general and consequently little grounded in fact. Moreover, and to our surprise, these two questions did not form a single factor for the white subsample (N=131).

Our attempt to develop a measure of national involvement must be considered a failure. It is important to ask why we failed. Four possible explanations seem worth consideration: 1) National involvement as an attitude producing human behavior does not exist: 2) The attitude does exist (at least for our black respondents) and is reflected in questions 2 and 3 (see Table 6-1); but national involvement is only one of many variables affecting reactions to specific historical problems such as the Vietnam War or conscientious objectors; 3) The instrument was poorly worded or conceived; for instance, the Vietnam question asked respondents whether they ever thought the war was not "worth fighting." Obviously, "worth" could be interpreted in several different ways, e.g., the war costs too much, the war is immoral, or the Vietnamese are not worth defending; and 4) It now seems likely to us that some of the questions were better measures of nationalism than national involvement. For instance, the Vietnam question is similar to asking people to admit they made a mistake; people can do this even about themselves provided they do not have an image of themselves as being perfect. A crusading nationalist might have such an image of the nation, and thus be unable to admit the nation erred, but someone can be involved with the nation and admit a mistake. Similarly, it seems to us that some of the other questions (especially the ones about spitting on the flag, people fighting for the country, and being scared by the Russians) are probably more related to personal maturity than involvement.

That six questions are interrelated suggests that it is possible that a sense of national involvement does really exist among our respondents. At least in part, the smallness of the interrelations reflects our inadequate reasoning as to the behavioral implications of national involvement. Future attempts to measure involvement by studying its supposed effects must be careful to sort out the effects of involvement, knowledge of specific historical events (like the Vietnam War), and the effects of respondents' immaturity. But the weakness of the correlations, also, casts doubt on the significance of a sense of national involvement in determining how the homemakers of Kilbourntown react to the events that occur around them.

The next section of this chapter will examine responses to one of the questions meant to measure national involvement: "How do you feel when you hear people say how great the United States is—angry, no different than usual, somewhat proud, or very proud?" Of the six questions just discussed this question seems closest to reflecting a sense of oneness with the nation. To feel anger would suggest negative involvement; to be proud would indicate positive involvement; to remain unchanged would suggest indifference. Although this question is obviously relevant to the topic of involvement, we cannot claim it is an adequate measure of involvement. It is too easy to give the "proud" responses. The question is biased in favor of positive involvement. On the other hand, we are not suggesting that people would lie to the interviewers. Most people no doubt believe themselves when they say they would feel proud, but probably more give this response than would actually feel proud if they heard someone praise the United States. The "nation question" is perhaps best understood as a measure of the respondent's self-perception of national involvement. As such it has some value.

FEELING PROUD ABOUT THE UNITED STATES

As noted above there were four responses to the question about how the respondent would feel if she heard people say how great the United States is: get angry, no different than usual, somewhat proud, or very proud. Only four people (two black, two white) chose "angry." This could be realistic on the level of self-consciousness; perhaps only four homemakers can readily admit to themselves that they are basically angered by the nation in which they reside. The small number could also reflect a desire to please our interviewers. At any rate we combined our first two categories into one labelled "indifference." Those who responded "somewhat proud" are labelled "moderate involvement" and those who said "very proud" are listed under "strong involvement."

When we defined national involvement as a sense of oneness with the nation we did not specify that the individual must like the nation. For us involvement can be positive or negative. Someone who loves the nation and another who hates it are equally involved with it. (On this point we differ from many "alienation" studies in which alienation is equated not with the absence of involvement but with the presence of negative involvement, i.e., involvement with a hated object). Given the fact that involvement can be positive or negative, it is especially regretable that we were not able to use our "get angry" category, which would have reflected negative involvement. It must be continually kept in mind that in this section the discussion is restricted to seemingly positive involvement. Moreover, at best our study reflects involvement at the conscious level in a form acceptable to the respondent. Given the turbulent racial situation in the United States it seems especially necessary to remember that an individual need not have only one sense of involvement. As psychoanalysts have taught us we must see the individual as having many layers of personality each of which may have its own sense of involvement. What our study reflects, assuming it is meaningful, is the sense of involvement as the person rather consciously decides to portray it in the public and somewhat formal situation of being interviewed.

AGE, COLOR, AND NATIONAL INVOLVEMENT

Table 6-2 presents the distribution of national-involvement scores by age and color. There is no consistent difference between whites and blacks. The main color difference appears among those sixty and over, in which age range the whites are somewhat more involved in the nation.

Age, on the other hand, does seem significant especially for the whites. There is a tendency for involvement to increase with age among the whites. The data are less clear for the blacks. Involvement and age seem curvilinearly related among the blacks. The percentage of "indifference," for instance, declines then rises. This is also true of the percentage of "strong involvement." A curvilinear pattern also appears in the "strong involvement" column for whites; the peak for "strong involvement" is in the fifty to fifty-nine age range. Overall, it can certainly be concluded that as people age they seem to be more involved with the nation than the very young, i.e., those in their twenties and thirties. But the data also suggest that national involvement declines in old age. The peak of involvement occurs in our sample among those in their fifties.

TABLE 6–2

NATIONAL INVOLVEMENT

(By age and color of respondent)

	White				Black			
Age[1]	Indif-ference	Moderate involve-ment	Strong involve-ment	Sample size (N)	Indif-ference	Moderate involve-ment	Strong involve-ment	Sample size (N)
22–29	36%	7%	57%	(14)	25%	18%	57%	(108)
30–39	26	8	66	(24)	25	20	55	(111)
40–49	19	12	69	(26)	13	17	70	(69)
50–59	10	10	81	(31)	15	3	82	(34)
60 and above	11	18	71	(63)	21	16	63	(38)
No re-sponse	—	—	—	(1)	—	—	—	(7)
Total				(159[2])				(367)

1. In this chapter the first age aggregate begins with age "twenty two" because we have restricted our sample to respondents who were of voting-age at the time of the 1964 national election (i.e., one and a half years prior to our study.)

2. Our white subsample in this chapter is 165, but 6 whites did not answer the national involvement question.

REGION AND NATIONAL INVOLVEMENT

We were surprised by the general lack of difference between races in terms of involvement. In all, 70 percent of the whites and 62 percent of the blacks are strongly involved in the nation. Our expectation was that blacks would be much less involved. In Chapter One we set forth the theory that involvement is a function of similarity, power, and knowledge. It seemed to us that whites would have more bases than blacks for feeling positively involved in the nation. Certainly the symbolic personalities of the nation are whites, so that blacks should feel less similar to the "nation" than whites. On the other hand there is some ambiguity regarding the power variable. Although both races are to a significant extent determined by governmental action, this process is much more direct (e.g., welfare services) for the black people, so that blacks might be more conscious of their dependence on the national government. With regard to knowledge we assumed that the whites would know more about the government (which in the United States is probably synonymous with the nation), and so be more involved. Overall, therefore, we expected whites to be more involved with the nation than blacks.

Moveover, in the case of black people it seems to us that there is some conflict between national involvement and loyalty to the black ethnic group. More and more black leaders seem to define the situation as one in which the more loyal you are to your color the less committed you should be to the national institutions and national leaders. "Black" involvement seems to militate against national involvement.

The appearance of the "black nationalism" movement has been accompanied by a renewed sense of brotherhood with black people everywhere. The self-assertion of black people has been accompanied not only by a stress on the separation of black people within the United States but also by an international orientation, at least among some of the leaders. There is a growing interest among black Americans in black people around the world. For instance, there is the use of African names and African styles of dress.

Even if the bases of involvement exist for black people, therefore, this potentiality might never be fully actualized. A prior or higher loyalty to race might prevent the growth of national involvement.

We expected black people to be less involved with the nation, therefore, both because of a relative absence of bases of involvement and because of the effects of their commitment to racial unity. We were very surprised, therefore, by the similarity of white and black respondents.

To explore racial differences further we subdivided the black population into three aggregates: those born in the northern states, those born in the border states, and those born in the southern states. There is little difference between northerners and border people; the percentages for strong national involvement are 50 percent and 49 percent respectively. On the other hand 67 percent of the southerners are high on national involvement.

Table 6-3 presents data on the relation between age, region of birth and national involvement. Considering black people only, age and region both seem significant, but region is the more important of the two. The highest percentage of people who said they would feel very proud occurs among the older black women born in the south.

Part B of the same table contains the scores for whites divided by age in the same manner as we divided the blacks. Comparing just those blacks and whites from the north and border states, there are fewer blacks high on

TABLE 6–3

NATIONAL INVOLVEMENT

(By region of birth, age, and color of respondent)

Region of birth and age	A. National involvement: Black			
	Indifference	Moderate involvement	Strong involvement	Sample size (N)
North and border states, 39 or below	29%	30%	41%	(59)
North and border states, 40 and above	20	24	56	(46)
Southern states, 39 or below	24	14	62	(159)
Southern states, 40 and above	14	9	77	(92)
				(356¹)

Region of birth and age	B. National involvement: White			
North and border states, 39 or below	39%	11%	50%	(38)
North and border states, 40 and above	13	14	73	(120)
				(158²)

1. Eleven cases were lost; four came from regions other than those reported above; seven did not report age.

2. In one case there was no response for age.

national involvement but there are more indifferent whites among those thirty-nine and below. The higher frequency of indifference among the young whites probably reflects that there are more truly alienated people among the young whites than among the young blacks in our sample. Just as in our analysis of the household we found white mothers who seemed truly uninvolved in every aspect of their environment, so now we similarly find more young white mothers indifferent to the nation. Of course, such people are a minority. We did not check to determine if the ignorant mothers are also indifferent citizens. But the evidence does suggest that the highest percentage of truly alienated people exist in our white sample.

If we compare the older whites with the older blacks from the north and border region a different picture emerges. The older whites are more involved in the nation. Clearly, among those forty and over and born in the northern and border states our expectation that whites would more frequently be highly involved in the nation than blacks is substantiated. However, the difference is not as dramatic as we might have expected.

But we must also compare the older whites with our black subsamples from the south. The older black women from the south and the older white women from the north are almost identical in their distribution of scores.

Why are older black women from the south so involved with the nation? The fact of southern origin seems important. Even among the young, black women from the south are more frequently strongly involved with the nation than young black women from the north. Being southern seems to mean being involved with the nation.

Stouffer in his study of civil liberties found southerners least tolerant of nonconformers, a fact not explainable in terms of rural-urban or educational differences among people from different regions. Stouffer writes: "There is something in Southern culture that tends to differentiate Southerners, in cities as well as rural areas, at all educational levels, from all other regional groups."[4] What is southern culture?

C. Vann Woodward believes that the distinctive history of the South gives this region a unique identity. Further, he suggests that a distinctive regional identity would protect southerners from extreme nationalism.[5] This may be true, but the evidence suggests that a part of this regional identity is national involvement, if not nationalism. Why might southerners more often be strong-ly involved in the nation? There is one aspect of Woodward's analysis of southern history that suggests an answer. Unlike other Americans, southerners are "concrete;" they are involved in specific places. Woodward quotes Eudora Welty as follows: "Like a good many other [regional] writers, I am myself touched off by place. The place where I am and the place I know, and other places that familarity with and love for... set me to writing my stories." "She speaks of 'the blessing of being located—contained' ".[6] It is possible that the sense of being rooted in a certain physical place contributes to national involvement. The sense of being located and of valuing a location might move people to identify with the symbolic representations of that place—the local community, the region, and the nation.

It is also possible that part of the southern heritage is militaristic, almost Prussian-like. If so, this would certainly favor the appearance not only of national involvement but nationalism.

The important point is that, for whatever reason, southern culture seems to explain the unexpectedly high national involvement in our black subsample. Northern blacks are less involved in the nation than northern whites. Of course, it is possible that southern whites are more involved in the nation than southern blacks. We want to stress, however, the apparent role of a regional culture in producing national involvement. We shall return to discuss the significance of southern culture for black people after more data are presented.

MASS MEDIA AND NATIONAL INVOLVEMENT

Karl Deutsch has stressed the point that a nation has a unique communication system, taken in the broad sense to include language, history, and actual exchange of information. "Membership in a people essentially consists in wide complementarity of social communication. It consists in the ability to communicate more effectively. and over a wider range of subjects, with members of one large group than with outsiders."[7]

However, he also notes that "to permit the rise of national consciousness, there must be a minimum, at least, of cohesion and distinctiveness of a people; and these must have acquired at least a minimum of importance in the lives of individuals."[8] Seemingly, communication is effective only if bases of involvement are already present. From the perspective of our theory of involvement the effect of communication *per se* is ambiguous.

The most immediate effect of communication should be greater knowledge and a sense of greater understanding. In terms of our study this should mean that people who use the mass media should become more conscious of the existence of a nation, should realize they have knowledge of this nation, and therefore should be more involved with the nation.

But will this involvement be positive or negative? National leaders pictured on television, for instance, will in almost all cases be white. What will be the reaction of black people? They might realize that American citizenship means dependence on white people, and hate their nation. Or, they could see that leaders such as John F. Kennedy stood for things they valued; realizing, then, that national leaders shared their goals, black people might feel more involved in their nation in a positive way. The mass media can make people realize their dependence on nonlocal events. But will this lead to simple

TABLE 6–4

TELEVISION NEWSCAST VIEWING AND NATIONAL INVOLVEMENT

(By color of respondent)

	National involvement							
Viewing of national television newscasts	White				Black			
	Indifference	Moderate	Strong	Sample size (N)	Indifference	Moderate	Strong	Sample size (N)
Don't watch Brinkley or Cronkite	24%	17%	59%	(41)	20%	18%	62%	(91)
Watch Brinkley and/or Cronkite	13	12	75	(118)	21	17	62	(276)
Totals				(159)				(367)

appreciation of a fact or to resentment? Will an awareness of dependence on a national government lead to positive or negative involvement?

There is no doubt that communication seems likely to increase involvement. But the fact of communication, itself, cannot tell us whether the resulting involvement will be positive or negative.

It is difficult, therefore, to predict the overall effect of mass media usage. Our expectation was that the increased information associated with such usage would lead to increased positive involvement. But especially in the case of the black people it it difficult to predict the overall consequence of media usage with any certitude.

In passing it should be noted that we studied two forms of communication: schooling and the mass media. Because it is a means of information-transmission we expected schooling to have effects similar to the mass media. Znaniecki stressed the importance of schooling in giving all children of a nation a common literature, history, set of culture-heroes, and ideology.[9] Unexpectedly we found no relation between years of schooling and national involvement, even after we controlled for age and region of birth. It could be that this outcome reflects the admitted crudeness of our national involvement measure or the absence of any measure of educational quality. The latter problem would seem especially important. But we believe that the effects of formal schooling, except with regard to the development of basic skills, is so superficial that later experience can easily modify the school experience.

Is there any relation between mass media usage and national involvement?

We asked our respondents if they had a television set, and if they did whether they usually watch several specific T.V. personalities. Among the names were Walter Cronkite and David Brinkley.[10] Table 6-4 shows the distribution of national involvement scores according to whether the respondent does or does not watch Brinkley or Cronkite. For whites there is a definite tendency toward strong involvement to be associated with newscast-watching. However, no similar relation appears for the blacks.

The same analysis was done for the black subsample, controlling for age and region of birth. But, generally the subgroups contained too few nonwatchers for meaningful analysis except in the case of the young, southern-born black people; no pattern between the two variables (i.e., media usage and national involvement) appears in this subsample. Television news seems to lack impact on national involvement for our black women.

However, the overwhelming preponderance of those who say they do watch news programs among the blacks must make us suspicious; 75 percent of our sample said they usually watch one or both of the news programs. It could be the people were simply lying. More likely it is a case of the television being on with nobody giving much attention to it as long as the news is on. It could be argued that we should have asked how often they watch news programs. But we thought that any contact with such an effective media as television would have an impact.

We also asked our respondents: "Do you have a chance to read any newspapers?" If they said "yes" we asked them which one and whether they read them "about every day, several times a week, or a couple of times a month." Note that this question puts more of a burden on the respondent than the television-news question. She must name the newspapers, and then answer the frequency question in terms of each named newspaper.

Table 6-5 presents the national involvement data according to the frequency of newspaper-reading. If the respondent read more than one newspaper, she was classified according to the highest frequency with which she read any one newspaper. Clearly, for the white people national involvement appears to be positively related to newspaper-reading. Because of sample-size problems we were not able to use all our reading-frequency categories. The analysis of the white subsample, however, does give some support to the idea that frequent involvement with the mass media is associated with positive national involvement.

The data for the black sample do not show this pattern. Newspaper-reading does not seem related to national involvement among our black respondents. Those who read a newspaper "a couple of times a month," however, deviate from everybody else; they are twice as frequently indifferent as the rest of the black sample. Of course, there are only few of these cases (N=27). But there seems to be a reasonable explanation for their relatively high frequency of indifference. It must be remembered that "a couple of times a month" is the lowest reading-frequency offered those who said they do get a chance to read the newspaper. It is quite possible that some of these respondents never read the newspaper more than two or three times a year. Still, why would they more often be indifferent than those who never read a newspaper? We suggest that those who never read a paper develop an alternative means of gathering information such as listening to the radio. On the other hand, those who chose the lowest reading-frequency category are those who do use the newspaper to find out what is happening in the world but who hardly ever bother to get this information. In short, it is possible that the people in the "couple of times a month" category do know least about the nation, so that their high frequency of indifference would be consistent with our expectation that information would increase positive involvement.

But, in general Table 6-5 suggests that frequency of newspaper-reading among black respondents is not significantly related to national involvement. To check this further we controlled for age and region of birth, then calculated the percentage that gave the "very proud" response. Table 6-6 presents these percentages for the black sample.

TABLE 6–5

NEWSPAPER READING FREQUENCY AND NATIONAL INVOLVEMENT

(By color of respondent)

	National involvement							
	White[1]				Black			
Frequency of reading daily newspapers	Indif- ference	Moderate	Strong	Sample size (N)	Indif- ference	Moderate	Strong	Sample size (N)
Daily	13%	13%	74%	(124)	21%	20%	59%	(170)
Several times a week					20	13	67	(106)
Couple of times a month	29	14	57	(35)	41	10	49	(27)
Don't read newspapers					19	14	67	(64)
Total				(159)				(367)

1. Because of small frequencies we combined, for the whites only all the reading categories except "daily."

TABLE 6-6

PERCENTAGE GIVING STRONG NATIONAL INVOLVEMENT RESPONSE

(By newspaper reading frequency, region of birth, and age of respondent for blacks)[1]

Newspaper-reading frequency	North and border region				Southern region			
	39 or below		40 and above		39 or below		40 and above	
	%	N	%	N	%	N	%	N
Daily	34	(32)	58	(26)	59	(70)	83	(40)
Several times a week	53	(15)	55	(11)	62	(50)	83	(24)
Couple of times a month	—	(5)	—	(2)	60	(15)	—	(5)
Don't read newspapers	—	(7)	—	(7)	71	(24)	65	(23)

1. There is a total sample of 356; 11 cases were lost because respondents come from different regions or did not report age.

First, let us consider age and region differences, In all but one case the older respondents are more often strongly involved in the nation; the exception occurs among the southern-born women who do not read any newspaper, among whom young and old are much alike. Consistently, the southern-born are often strongly involved in the nation. Both age and birth-place, therefore, remain related to national involvement.

Second, let us consider the impact of newspaper-reading frequency by looking down each column. Looking at the black women born outside the south, there are usually only a few cases in each cell of the table, but it is interesting to note that the young daily readers stand out from the other subgroups because of the relative infrequency of strong national involvement. Among young non-southerners, then, frequent newspaper-reading seems associated with the absence of national involvement.

A somewhat similar process occurs among the young southern-born black women. In this subgroup strong involvement occurs most often among those who do not read any newspaper, but the difference between daily readers and nonreaders is only 12 percent. On the other hand, there is a stronger tendency in the reverse direction among the older southern-born women. In this subgroup our expectations about the effect of exposure to newspapers is supported. However, among the young reading the newspaper seems associated, although weakly, with the absence of strong involvement. This suggests that the more the young women learn about what is going on, the less often they identify with the nation.

Our ideas concerning the influence of the mass media seem to fit the white respondents' behavior. But among the black women television-news watching is insignificant, and the effects of newspaper-reading are not consistently in the same direction. Yet the fact that most surprised us is the strong national involvement of the southern-born black women.

If anybody in our total sample has a right to hate the United States it is the southern black person. These people have been deprived of their civil and human rights. Yet they have high national involvement (the reader must remember that in this discussion involvement means positive involvement). For the southern negro, culture seems to drown out experience. We cannot imagine that there are more bases in the experience of southern blacks for them to feel national involvement than there are in the life of northern blacks. Southern black involvement seems artificial, something implanted by cultural agents but lacking any roots in the daily experience of the black respondents.

The argument might be made that northern black people are affected by relative deprivation. Because northerners expect more, they are more easily frustrated. As a result they have a less positive attitude toward the national government. This may be sound reasoning, but it does not tell us why southern black people should feel a strong positive involvement with the nation.

It is true that the question used to measure national involvement reflects only the respondent's conscious image of her involvement. But for whites this image seems to be meaningful, i.e., it is related in the expected manner to a possible basis in experience for national involvement. On the other hand, among the black respondents this image seems to mirror not experience with the nation but regional culture. The pattern of black involvement does not seem justified by experience; the pattern seems to be the result of a culture unthinkingly passed on from generation to generation, which has produced a people whose verbal reactions are divorced from their experience.

Our data suggest that among the black respondents there exists a subtle form of self-alienation. Southern culture seems to have produced people whose conscious image of themselves does not seem justified in their daily experience. What are the consequences of this form of self-alienation? This is a question for future research.

Since we question the meaningfulness of the involvement question for our black respondents, it seemed inappropriate to continue the analysis on national involvement using this question. If the response to this question does not seem to be justified by the black person's actual experiences, then the answer probably tells us little about the extent to which the nation serves as a source of order in the daily lives of our black respondents. If the answer is artificial, it would not be an accurate indicator of the extent to which our respondents orient their lives by national goals and by their role as citizens.

The rest of this chapter will be concerned with voting in the 1964 presidential election (Johnson versus Goldwater). Voting in an election is not an adequate measure of national involvement. On the other hand, it is a sign that a person does orient her life through her role as a citizen. We are not interested in the candidate or person supported, but whether people voted. Our concern is not to label people as "liberal" or "conservative," but as "involved" or "uninvolved." Voting is an indication that a person is involved in the nation. It is not a measure of involvement but a sign of involvement.

NATIONAL INVOLVEMENT AND VOTING

Voting is one of the most studied aspects of human behavior. In the course of all this research voting has been found to be related to a host of variables. Stokes divides these variables into three types: 1) Voting is normative, i.e., people vote because they are supposed to; voting is a good thing in itself in American culture. On the other hand, one reason women might not vote is because the norm is less applicable to them than to men; 2) Voting is instrumental, i.e., people vote because voting is a means to some desired goal. Obviously a great variety of goals might be relevant to political action, which means that the actual immediate motivations for the voting will be quite diverse, making empirical study difficult. On the other hand, people might lack self-confidence or feel that the situation is hopeless, or that the right result is assured even without their vote, and so not participate in the election; or the instrumental act might not occur because a person is pulled in different directions by different goals, and the resulting tension might be resolved by withdrawal from the situation; 3) Voting is expressive. By this Stokes seems to mean that the act of voting might become symbolically connected with nonpolitical objects; so, for instance, someone might refrain from voting because his hated father is a politician, and not voting is a means of hurting him. This brief summary suggests the variety of variables that could be considered in any analysis of voting. We shall be limited in our approach and consider only a few relevant variables.[11]

Stokes's "expressive" category refers to voting as a symbolic act. We would expect that those who are highly involved in the nation would be motivated to express this involvement by voting. One pressure to vote, therefore, would be to express national involvement.

This theory assumes that involvement seeks to express itself. As commonsensical as our argument might sound, there is in fact no truly obvious reason why national involvement must express itself in voting. However, we do think there should be such a relationship, i.e., we do suggest that if people feel involved, and if they are offered an opportunity to express this involvement, they will accept it. There are two lines of argument why this might be so. First, it might be that a sense of involvement loses its significance if not expressed

TABLE 6–7

NATIONAL INVOLVEMENT AND PERCENTAGE VOTING

	(By color of respondent)			
	Percentage voting			
National involvement	White		Black	
	%	N	%	N
Indifference	42	(26)	47	(79)
Moderate involvement	66	(21)	59	(59)
Strong involvement	57	(112)	57	(225)
Total		(159)		(363)[1]

1. In four cases the respondent did not answer the voting question.

in overt action. People might seek to express or concretize their involvement in order to give reality to this feeling. This interpretation suggests that people seek out opportunities to express their involvements. Second, it might be that if a person is presented with an opportunity to act out a sense of involvement, and fails to act, this abstention would imply that the person is not involved; and to avoid the tension that would result from the apparent inconsistency of being involved but acting as if not involved, the more involved people would vote. There seems ample reason, then, for suggesting a relation between national involvement and voting.

Table 6-7 presents the relevant data. There is some modest support here for our theory. Indifferent respondents vote least often among both whites and blacks. On the other hand there is little difference between the other two degrees of national involvement. That the difference between the percentage voting among the indifferent respondents and the percentages for the two categories of involvement is greater among the whites is consistent with our argument that black involvement is artificial.

The association between national involvement and voting supports the idea that voting is a sign of involvement. Some people might argue, however, that no contemporary presidential election has offered a meaningful choice, so that voting has little significance. This may be true. It follows, then, that some people who are highly involved in the nation may choose not to vote because they view this act as trivial. We assume such people are few in Kilbourntown. Our purpose in the next section is to determine through an analysis of voting which people in Kilbourntown orient their lives to a national social order. Since Americans are expected to vote only once or twice a year, someone could

TABLE 6-8

PERCENTAGE VOTING

	(By age and color of respondent)			
	Percentage voting			
Age	*White*		*Black*	
	%	*N*	*%*	*N*
22–29	—	(10)	36	(105)
30–39	52	(25)	56	(112)
40–49	50	(26)	61	(71)
50–59	69	(33)	64	(34)
60–74	60	(48)	78	(37)
75 plus	30	(20)	—	(2)
No response	—	(3)	—	(7)
Total		(165)		(368)

vote at every opportunity and spend most of his life unconcerned about the nation. Sudying voting is only a crude substitute for what is needed—a measure of the extent to which daily life or at least major decisions are influenced by national goals. Until such a measure is developed, analyses of voting may be useful in suggesting conditions that foster an orientation to the national social order.

VOTING

Table 6-8 presents the percentage voting by age and color. Two aggregates stand out: the old whites and the young blacks. That fewer young people vote than middle-aged people seems generally true.[12] But the analysis of national data by Glenn and Grimes does not support the idea that old people are less likely to vote than the middle-aged; 90 percent of the people interviewed in the research reported by Glenn and Grimes who were seventy to seventy-nine years old voted in the 1964 election.[13] Apparently the elderly white ladies of Kilbourntown are far from representative of their age cohort. They are much more alienated than the typical elderly person. Of course, the age range of the elderly women we interviewed went higher than seventy-nine; but it seems unlikely that the difference between 30 percent (the percent voting in our study) and 90 percent (the percent voting in research reported by Glenn and Grimes) can be explained by the difference in the age ranges. The elderly white ladies in Kilbourntown cannot be considered representative of people their age.

TABLE 6–9

VIEWING OF NATIONAL TELEVISION NEWSCASTS AND PERCENTAGE VOTING

(By color of respondent)

Viewing of national television newscasts	Percentage voting			
	White		Black	
	%	N	%	N
Don't own television	40	(15)	33	(18)
Own a television, don't watch newscasts	54	(28)	44	(73)
Watch Brinkley and/or Cronkite	60	(122)	58	(277)
Total		(165)		(368)

Between thirty and seventy-four years of age the pattern is different for whites and for blacks. Among the former there seems to be a curvilinear relation between age and the percentage voting, while among the black respondents there seems to be a linear, positive relationship. Such different patterns prevent any conclusion about the relation of aging to national involvement.

Generally, the percentages are higher for the black respondents. The most striking difference is among those sixty to seventy-four years old, among whom the blacks have a much higher voting percentage.

It might be argued that our failure to eliminate those who could not vote because of residency requirements might account for the low percentage of young black voters. But among those black women in their twenties who have lived in Milwaukee five years or less, 28 percent voted, while among those who have lived in Milwaukee six to ten years, 34 percent voted. If residency was a major explanation for the low percentage of voters we would expect a large difference between these two subsamples.

Using voting as a sign of national involvement, we can say that among the young and the old the nation seems of little relevance. For the rest of the sample at least the majority voted.

What influences people to orient their lives to the state?

MASS MEDIA AND VOTING

It seems probable that those people who make use of the mass media will vote. It has been found that people with more political knowledge are more likely to vote.[14] Knowledge can motivate voting in at least two ways: 1) Knowledge is a source of involvement. Learning about the nation, therefore, would increase national involvement and people involved with the nation are likely to express their involvement by voting; 2) Knowledge helps people to understand how their goals are related to national programs, and people who have this understanding are more likely to vote. Because the mass media transmit political knowledge, especially in their news programs, and because such knowledge is related to voting, it seems probable that media involvement is also related to voting.

Table 6-9 presents data on television-news watching and voting. For both whites and blacks more of those who watch the newscasts voted. However, among the whites there is little difference between those who own a television but do not watch newscasts and those who do watch them. These two aggregates are quite different among the blacks. The evidence suggests, therefore, that news programs are more significant for blacks than whites.

Table 6-10 presents data on newspaper-reading frequency and voting. There is again a positive relation between mass media involvement and the voting-percentage, and again the relationship is stronger for blacks than for whites. The only deviance from our expectations is that the "couple of times a month" readers are lower even than the nonreaders. But this is consistent with our previous discussion of who is likely to use the "couple of times a month" response. As the reader will recall, the people choosing this response showed the least involvement in the nation on the basis of the "nation" question.

In general, mass media involvement is positively related to voting percentage, but this relationship is stronger for the black sample. This is similar to the finding of Matthews and Prothro that exposure to the mass media is associated with a greater increase in political participation among southern blacks than among southern whites.[15]

But is it that media involvement itself is important, or is it that other variables motivate people both to learn about their environment and to vote, without their being any direct connection between this learning and voting? As would be expected among the black respondent: 1) more of those born in the north (71 percent) voted, than those born in the border states (54 percent) or in the south (52 percent); 2) more of those born in a city (70 percent) voted than those born in a small city (55 percent), a town (59 percent), or on a farm (49 percent). However, when we compared our black respondents who had had one to eight years of schooling with those who had had more, we found no

TABLE 6–10

NEWSPAPER READING FREQUENCY AND PERCENTAGE VOTING

(By color of respondent)

Newspaper-reading frequency[1]	Percentage voting			
	White		Black	
	%	N	%	N
Daily	59	(130)	67	(170)
Several times a week	53	(17)	53	(103)
Couple of times a month	—	(7)	30	(28)
Don't read newspapers	45	(11)	40	(67)
Total		(165)		(368)

1. This is based on how frequently the respondent read either of the two major daily newspapers: the Journal and the Sentinel. If the respondent read both, but with different frequencies, the higher frequency was used in assigning the respondent to a category.

difference; in both aggregates 54 percent voted. We decided to form subsamples based on region of birth. urbanness (people were divided into those born in a large city and everyone else), and age. Table 6-11 presents the subsamples and the percentage of each who voted. The range of percentages (30-84 percent) is quite dramatic. The young, nonurban, southern-born stand out as nonvoters. All three variables—region, urbanness, age—seeem to be significant. Is media involvement related to voting percentage within these subsamples?

Table 6-12 shows the relation between newspaper-reading frequency and voting percentage within four subsamples. The northern and the southern urban subsamples are combined because of the small frequencies of each type. Although some of the cells in Table 6-12 are quite small, the pattern is the same as in Table 6-10. Media involvement is positively related to voting percentage.

An analysis similar to that in Table 6-12 except involving television-newscast watching showed that this variable continued to be related to voting percentage even within subsamples.

In a way our results seem to be too good. This is especially true with regard to newspaper-reading. Why is there a difference between people who read a paper "daily" and those who read it "several times a week"? Between national elections both groups must pick up plenty of information about national events. Why, then, are they different in voting percentages? Similarly, we found that more of those people who read two newspapers voted than of those who reported reading only one. Is there not a saturation point for

TABLE 6–11

PERCENTAGE VOTING, CONTROLLING FOR REGION OF BIRTH,
URBANNESS OF BIRTHPLACE, AND AGE

		(For blacks)		
Region	Urbanness[1]	Age	Percentage voting	
			%	N
North	——	less than 30	62	(13)
North	——	30 and above	84	(31)
South	urban	less than 30	64	(14)
South	urban	30 and above	73	(22)
South	non-urban	less than 30	30	(76)
South	non-urban	30 and above	59	(199)
Total				(355)[2]

1. All those born in the North were considered to come from an urban environment.

2. Five voters and eight non-voters are excluded from failure to report age, region, or degree of urbanness; or because they do not come from the regions listed.

politically relevant information? Can the people who read two newspapers learn that much more than those who read only one? Table 6-12 suggests that there are just 3 significant groupings from the perspective of voting: those that read papers daily, those who say they read a "couple of times a month," and the rest, i.e., the people who responded either "several times a week" or "don't read;" their voting percentages are similar in the two subsamples in which we had enough cases to compare the aggregates. It is possible that many of the "don't read" respondents simply cannot read. For them reading is out as a source of information. But it is conceivable that for some of them their level of interest is high enough that they seek out information about the world in which they live from sources other than newspapers. As already suggested the "couple of times a month" respondents would be people who could and do read, but rarely because of their lack of interest in their environment.

But why is there such a difference between "daily" readers and the others, and especially why is there such a difference between "daily" readers and those who read the papers "several times a week"? We suggest that the choice of a frequency category is related to content of what is read. "Daily" readers would be people who read all the paper, while the other readers would be more selective, reading either the sports section, or the fashion section, or certain sensational stories or the like. We do not have the data to test this suggestion. However, based on our personal experience it seems plausible.

We suggest, therefore, that we have three aggregates: 1) those who read

TABLE 6–12

NEWSPAPER READING FREQUENCY AND PERCENTAGE VOTING
WITHIN FOUR RELATIVELY HOMOGENEOUS SUBSAMPLES THAT
EMERGED FROM CONTROLLING FOR REGION OF BIRTH,
URBANNESS OF BIRTHPLACE, AND AGE OF RESPONDENT

	(For Blacks)							
	Percentage voting							
Frequency of reading daily newspaper	*South, non-urban, less than 30*		*South, non-urban, 30 and above*		*North; South urban; less than 30*		*North; South urban; 30 and above*	
	%	*N*	*%*	*N*	*%*	*N*	*%*	*N*
Daily	39	(23)	69	(98)	69	(13)	87	(31)
Several times a week	25	(24)	54	(50)	—	(9)	75	(16)
Couple of times a month	—	(8)	27	(14)	—	(3)	—	(2)
Don't read news-papers	28	(21)	49	(37)	—	(2)	—	(4)
Total		(76)		(199)		(27)		(53)

"daily" and read all the news; 2) those who read the newspaper rarely; such individuals use the newspaper as a source of information but so rarely that it does not motivate them to political participation; and 3) the rest—a composite made up of people who do not read but use other media, as well as those who read the papers but do so selectively. This third aggregate occasionally becomes aware of politically relevant information, and thus some of them are motivated to vote, depending on the interplay of a host of forces.

The television question did not ask about frequency of watching, so we can not adequately compare our different categories on the television and newspaper questions.

VOLUNTARY ASSOCIATION AND VOTING

Numerous studies have found that those who belong to voluntary associations are more politically active.[16] McClosky argues that this relation between membership and political activity occurs because: 1) experience in association makes people more articulate; 2) it increases their sensitivity to the relation between their self-interest and political events; and 3) membership means exposure to agencies of socialization, which will reinforce the sense of civic duty.[17] Seeman's work reinforces the idea that participation in associations

TABLE 6–13

MEMBERSHIP IN VOLUNTARY ASSOCIATIONS AND PERCENTAGE
VOTING

(By color of respondent)				
Voluntary association membership	Percentage voting			
	White		Black	
	%	N	%	N
Non-member	48	(104)	44	(185)
Membership in one associa- tion	71	(41)	63	(124)
Two or more memberships	75	(20)	77	(59)
		(165)	(368)	

would increase self-confidence. Specifically, he found that absence of membership in organizations is associated with a general sense of powerlessness.[18] Finally, participation in associations means exposure to a greater variety of interpersonal influences than would be found among family and close friends, so that if a person has any inclination to vote, she would be more likely to find social support for this action if she is a member of formal organizations.

In this section, we shall: 1) consider whether there is evidence to support the significance of voluntary associations for our sample, and 2) try to determine if media involvement is important, after controlling for association membership.

Table 6-13 relates organization membership and number of memberships to voting. "Voluntary association" in this analysis refers to: fraternal organizations, social clubs, veterans' organizations, community-improvement groups, labor unions, civil rights groups, church-related groups (but not church membership itself), P.T.A. or "Home and School," and political organizations. Each respondent was asked if she is a member of each type of organization just enumerated; in addition, there was a general question about whether she was a member of any other organization. The data in Table 6-13 shows the expected positive relation between association membership and voting.

Among the whites the number of memberships is less important than for our black respondents. Among the latter there is a significant difference between those belonging to only one organization and those belonging to two or more. This suggests that the white respondents are more disposed to vote and require fewer additional motivating forces in their environment before they are moved to vote.

TABLE 6–14

THE FREQUENCY OF ATTENDANCE AT VOLUNTARY ASSOCIATION MEETINGS AND PERCENTAGE VOTING

(By color of respondent)

Frequency of attendance at voluntary association meetings	Percentage voting			
	White		Black	
	%	N	%	N
Frequent	81	(26)	77	(75)
Occasional	78	(14)	64	(50)
Rare	57	(12)	55	(18)
Non-member	48	(104)	42	(187)
Total		(156)[1]		(330)[1]

1. Nine whites and thirty eight blacks did not report frequency.

We would expect that if the processes suggested by McClosky are important, then voting percentage should be related not only to membership but also to frequency of attendance at organizational meetings. For each organization the respondent was asked whether she attended meetings "frequently," "occa-

TABLE 6–15

MEMBERSHIP IN VOLUNTARY ASSOCIATIONS AND PERCENTAGE VOTING WITHIN FOUR RELATIVELY HOMOGENEOUS SUBSAMPLES THAT EMERGED FROM CONTROLLING FOR REGION OF BIRTH, URBANNESS OF BIRTHPLACE, AND AGE OF RESPONDENT

(For blacks)

Voluntary association membership	Percentage voting							
	I South, non-urban, less than 30		II South, non-urban, 30 and above		III North; South urban; less than 30		IV North; South urban; 30 and above	
	%	N	%	N	%	N	%	N
Member	39	(38)	70	(92)	83	(12)	88	(33)
Non-member	21	(38)	49	(107)	47	(15)	65	(20)
Total		(76)		(199)		(27)		(53)

SOLIDARITY IN A SLUM

TABLE 6–16

NEWSPAPER-READING FREQUENCY,VOLUNTARY ASSOCIATION MEMBERSHIP, AND PERCENTAGE VOTING

	(By color of respondent)							
	Percentage voting							
	White				*Black*			
Frequency of reading daily newspapers	*Association member*		*Non-member*		*Association member*		*Non-member*	
	%	*N*	*%*	*N*	*%*	*N*	*%*	*N*
Daily	70	(52)	50	(78)	74	(104)	56	(66)
Several times or don't read	—	(6)	50	(22)	61	(72)	39	(98)
Couple of times a month	—	(3)	—	(4)	—	(7)	29	(21)
		(61)		(104)		(183)		(185)

sionally" or "rarely." In categorizing a respondent we used the single highest reported frequency for the organizations of which she is a member. Thus, if a respondent belongs to two organizations and attends one "frequently," but the other only "occasionally" she was categorized as a frequent attender for purposes of our analysis. Table 6-14 shows the relation between frequency of attendance and voting percentage. For the blacks especially there is a smooth, consistent increase in percentage voting as frequency of attendance increases. For the whites there is a basically similar pattern, although there is a tendency for the whites to dichotomize into frequent and occasional attenders versus the rest.

In Table 6-15 we compare members and nonmembers among the black respondents, controlling for age, region of birth, and urbanness of birth place. A difference of about 20 percent occurs within each subsample between members and nonmembers.

MASS MEDIA, VOLUNTARY ASSOCIATION MEMBERSHIP, AND VOTING

It is quite conceivable that those who read the newspapers frequently are also the people who belong to organizations. Is each of these variables independently associated with voting, or is it only one of them that affects political participation? Table 6-16 presents data on newspaper-reading frequency, as-

TABLE 6–17

NEWSPAPER-READING FREQUENCY, VOLUNTARY ASSOCIATION
MEMBERSHIP, AND PERCENTAGE VOTING FOR BLACK
RESPONDENTS BORN IN THE NON-URBAN SOUTH AND THIRTY
YEARS OR MORE OF AGE

Frequency of reading daily newspaper	Percentage voting			
	Association member		Non-member	
	%	N	%	N
Daily	75	(51)	64	(47)
Several times or don't read	69	(36)	39	(51)
Couple of times a month	—	(5)	—	(9)
		(92)		(107)

sociational membership, and voting percentage. For the white subsample, reading frequency seems unimportant, since both categories of reading frequency in the nonmember column have the same percentage of voters. However, association membership does seem important; there is a 20 percent difference between members and nonmembers among "daily" readers. It is also interesting that 85 percent of the white association members are "daily" readers. Among both whites and blacks we have an example of the 'piling on' process, i.e., those who are association members, and thus likely to vote, are disproportionately also "daily" readers. On the other hand, the percentages for the black subsamples support the conclusion that both reading frequency and association membership are significant. The lowest percentage is for the "couple of times - nonmember" category (29 percent), followed by the "several times/don't read - nonmember" category (39 percent). Appropriately, the highest percentage is for the "daily-member" cell (74 percent). Reading across the table and reading down the table, significant differences appear. The range of percentages (29-74 percent) is also impressive.

Why does reading frequency appear to be a more meaningful variable for the black respondents than for the white subsample? Among the whites 79 percent report reading the newspaper "daily," while only 46 percent of our black respondents said they read that often. Whites more than blacks are raised and live in an environment where newspapers are routinely bought and perused. Whites develop a habit of newspaper buying, but not all who buy read carefully through the paper. On the other hand, black people buy a newspaper regularly less out of habit and more because they want to read it. We are

TABLE 6–18

TELEVISION-NEWS WATCHING8 VOLUNTARY ASSOCIATION
MEMBERSHIP AND PERCENTAGE VOTING

(For blacks)

Viewing of national television newscasts	Percentage voting			
	Association member		Non-member	
	%	N	%	N
Watch Brinkley and/or Cronkite	73	(144)	47	(135)
Own a television, but don't watch newscasts	50	(32)	41	(39)
Don't own television	—	(7)	36	(11)
		(183)		(185)

suggesting that our reading-frequency categories more faithfully represent information-absorption among the blacks than among the whites. When a white person says she reads the newspaper daily this may mean little more than she buys it everyday. From the point of view of our theory, then, our questions probably are more meaningful among the blacks, for whom both media usage and association membership appear significant.

Table 6-17 is the same as the preceding table except we have limited our sample to those black women born in the nonurban South and thirty or more years of age, which is our largest subsample. Within this subsample reading frequency seems less important, than in the previous table, among association members. However, it is quite significant among non-members. Both media usage and association membership appear significant even in this subsample.

The analysis of the combined effects of television-news watching and organizational membership also tends to support the argument that both variables are significant. Tables 6-18 and 6-19 present the relevant data; both in our total black sample (the distribution of cases did not allow a meaningful analysis of whites) and in the subsample of nonurban, southern born, older women, percentages increase if the respondent watches the news and if she belongs to at least one association.

To evaluate the relative effect of newspaper reading and television watching let us compare Tables 6-17 and 6-19. The former table reveals that reading frequency is mainly important among the nonmembers, and that association membership has a greater effect among those who are not daily readers. Table

TABLE 6–19

TELEVISION-NEWS WATCHING, VOLUNTARY ASSOCIATION MEMBERSHIP, AND PERCENTAGE VOTING FOR BLACKS BORN IN THE NON-URBAN SOUTH AND THIRTY YEARS OF AGE OR MORE

Viewing of national television newscasts	Percentage voting			
	Association member		Non-member	
	%	N	%	N
Watch Brinkley and/or Cronkite	75	(72)	51	(80)
Others[1]	50	(20)	41	(27)
		(92)		(107)

1. This includes those who don't own a television and those who own one but do not watch Brinkley or Cronkite.

6-19 reveals that television has a bigger impact among association members, and that associational membership mainly effects those who watch the news. Looking at Table 6-19 it seems that television and membership have a significant impact only when they work together, i.e., among those who watch the news and belong to at least one organization. By themselves television and membership each increase voting percentage by about 10 percent only. On the other hand, newspapers seem able to have an independent effect. In fact, their main impact is among those who are nonmembers. In short, it seems as if there are two distinct processes that furnish the information that motivates people to vote: 1) watching television-newscasts and joining organizations, and 2) reading the newspaper daily.

If we might speculate further, we would suggest that these processes are associated with different types of voters. The second process, daily newspaper-reading, would suggest a more individualistic voter; someone who digests information alone. She is someone free to choose what to read and how to interpret it. Such a person might, also, change perspective less often because she is able to selectively perceive only what reinforces her present position. On the other hand, someone who receives information from television and from fellow organizational members is less able to control the flow of information and the process of interpretation. Such an individual would be more fluctuating in political behavior and more subject to social manipulation. But these ideas represent tentative hypotheses for further investigation.

Why is it that television-news watching and associational membership seems to be weak influences except when they are combined? If the effect of membership was to increase self-confidence or articulateness, we would expect this variable to have an impact independent of television, since the television-watching is not likely to increase confidence or articulateness. The most likely explanation for their weak influence as separate variables is that both are having their main impact through information-transmittal, but that neither gives sufficient information by itself for people to see the relation between their problems and political action.

It could be argued that the main variable producing voting is socialization, and that television simply reinforces the social obligation to vote, which is also supported by voluntary organizations. But it seems likely that the major part of socialization takes place through interpersonal contact, and therefore if a sense of civic duty is the main motive for voting, organizational membership should show a greater significance than it does.

If information-transmittal is the key variable affecting voting, then the type of organization a person belongs to should be related to voting. Following are several types of organizations our black respondents belonged to, the percentage of members who voted, and the total number of members in each organizational type: church-related groups—64 percent (N=65); P.T.A.—68 percent voted (N=109); civil rights groups—88 percent voted (N=19). The high percentage of voters in the civil rights groups makes sense, but we expected more P.T.A. members to vote than church-group members. However, it must be remembered that, as mentioned in the last chapter, P.T.A. members have poor attendance records. Moreover, some P.T.A. groups are no more than social clubs, while some religious leaders are political activists.

Other studies have found no relation between type of voluntary association and political behavior or attitudes.[19] There are two facts, then, that suggest that membership in voluntary associations is itself not an important variable. These facts are: 1) that type of organization is not important, and 2) in our study, that organizational membership has its main effect only in conjunction with television-news watching (see Table 6-18). On the other hand, that among television-news watchers a much higher percentage of association members voted suggests that organizations can channel the concern of people already interested in their environment into the field of politics.

To summarize: we have tried to study the political significance of the mass media and organizational membership. Our arguments have stressed that both are sources of information that, for several reasons, can motivate interest in the state. The data suggest two distinct information flows—one via daily newspaper-reading, the other via more public occasions for receiving information, such as at group meetings or from television newscasts, which often are watched with others. It is possible that these two processes are associated with two quite different types of political participants. What is most important for

TABLE 6–20

AGE OF RESPONDENT, YEARS IN MILWAUKEE, AND THE
PERCENTAGE VOTING

Age	Percentage voting			
	(For blacks)			
	0–15 years in Milwaukee		16 years or more in Milwaukee	
	%	N	%	N
22–29	35	(90)	67	(15)
30–39	51	(84)	71	(28)79
40–49	50	(34)	71	(35)
50–59	60	(15)	68	(19)
60 and over	72	(18)	86	(21)
		(241)		(118¹)

1. Nine cases were lost; eight of these failed to report age, while one did not report years in Milwaukee,

our purposes, however, is to affirm that media usage and organizational membership both are related to people using the nation as a point of orientation in their lives. The analysis of voting suggests that national involvement is related to both media involvement and associational membership.

However, it is possible that the relation, for instance, between media involvement and voting is due—not to one causing the other—but to the fact that both are related to another variable not included in our study. Only further research can eliminate this possibility.

MOBILITY AND VOTING

On the one hand, it could be argued that no matter where people move, they remain in the United States, so that mobility should not affect voting. Moreover, the mass media carry the same news all over the country, and many voluntary associations are national in scope, so that even if people move, they remain in the same national information network. On the other hand, moving poses problems such as having to reregister to vote and the like. But, more important from our point of view, the question arises whether in order for a national government to appear relevant a person must have roots and relationships in the local environment. Does a person who moves have a sense of somehow drifting above or outside of political systems? Is it difficult for someone to think of an act like voting as being personally relevant if the individual is not involved in the local community?

TABLE 6–21

YEARS IN MILWAUKEE AND THE PERCENTAGE VOTING

(For blacks 22–39 years old)		
Years in Milwaukee	Percentage voting	
	%	N
0–5	31	(62)
6–10	41	(56)
11–15	57	(57)
16 and over	70	(43)

Table 6-20 shows the difference in voting percentages between those who lived in Milwaukee fifteen years or less and the rest, controlling for age. Consistently more voting occurred among the age aggregates longer in residence.[20]

Table 6-21 presents a more refined analysis of years in Milwaukee for the black subpopulation twenty-two to thirty-nine years of age. The effects of mobility seem to wear off at different speeds for different individuals. There is no sharp dividing point below which we see the effects of mobility, and above which they have disappeared. Rather, the increase in voting percentage is gradual and continuous. The data suggest that participation in national affairs seems related to the development of local relationships.

This, of course, is consistent with our finding that voluntary association membership is a significant variable. The question arises whether the fact of membership in formal organizations or the degree to which any form of relationship has been developed is the crucial variable. To answer this question we divided our black sample into those twenty-two to twenty-nine and those thirty and over. Each subsample was further divided into those who are voluntary association members and those who are not. We then examined the relation between length of stay in Milwaukee and voting. Overall, both length of residence and association membership remained significant. In all subsamples a higher percentage of the more stable residents voted; similarly, holding constant length of residence, there still remained a difference in voting percentage, depending on whether the respondent was an association member or not. To compare the extremes, among the young, nonmember newcomers (in Milwaukee five years or less) 30 percent (N=23) while 82 percent (N=63) of the older, more stable (in Milwaukee sixteen years or more) association members voted. In the more detailed analysis, then, both length of residence and organizational affiliation retained significance.

The data, therefore, are consistent with the idea that national political participation, at least in the form of voting, is dependent on the degree of involvement in local relationships.

This evidence suggests the interesting idea that the expression of involvement in any social unit might be related to the degree of involvement in the immediate environment. Action, in general, may be affected by the degree to which we experience life as real. When does life become like reading a novel? When does the distinction between reality and fantasy become unimportant? We suggest that to the extent we are not involved in the environment of our daily life, a newspaper becomes a novel, and we lose the sense of urgency necessary for action. Perhaps involvement "in the environment of our daily life" is necessary to make life real.

CONCLUSION

We began this chapter by asking two questions: How involved are our respondents in the nation? What produces this involvement?

If we assume that both voting in the 1964 presidential election and giving the "strong involvement" response to the nation question are indicators of some national involvement, then a little over 80 percent of the sample is to some extent involved in the nation. Only 14 percent of the whites and 19 percent of the blacks neither voted nor chose the "strong involvement" response. We contacted only about 82 percent of the total number of households in Kilbourntown during our study. Possibly the people we could not reach are the less involved residents of K-3, but it is also conceivable that we could not contact these people because they were so busy outside their house in social activities like working, visiting, or going to meetings. Overall, there are surprisingly few people in Kilbourntown who do not indicate some involvement with the nation.

Certainly, it can not be said that our respondents live out their lives only in a world of personal relations. True isolation from the larger world would mean that the respondents would not vote, watch television newscasts or belong to any voluntary association. Only 8 percent of the sample fits this description. On the other hand, 29 percent did vote, watch television news, and belong to at least one voluntary association. The homemakers of Kilbourntown are generally in touch with a world that goes beyond their family.

As to what produces involvement we have stressed, following Deutsch, the importance of the flow of information. We assumed that if people receive information about national events they would be involved with the nation. Specifically, we studied the relation between mass media involvement and voting. The effect of these media seems to be greater among the black respondents. It seems likely to us that the stress on civic duty is much more important in white culture than black culture, so that information can have a greater impact among the black respondents. In other words, we are suggesting that voting among whites must be seen as not necessarily indicating anything more than artificial involvement. Whites vote and southern-born blacks have a self-image as involved people because their cultures support such behavior. Among both whites and blacks there are signs of an artificial national involvement not rooted in experience but culture.

Overall, the data support the ideas that: 1) exposure to information about national events increases national involvement, and 2) the mass media and voluntary associations seem to be significant sources of such information in Kilbourntown.

7

Conclusion

In Chapter One we elaborated on the experience of involvement. It is caused by closeness (although as previously noted, some of the data cast doubt on the significance of this variable), similarity, power, and knowledge. Moreover, the sense of oneness is heightened by overlap between fantasy and the sensed environment. In Chapters Three and Four we discussed different reasons for a lack of such an overlap. Throughout the first chapter the stress was on delineating in an abstract manner the social conditions that would produce an experience of oneness. This chapter guided our work. But a shift of focus began in chapter four. That chapter concluded with a section on the natural history of familial involvement. Time entered our analysis. The questions arose: How does the degree of involvement and the bases of involvement change over time in our relations with the same objects? What are the consequences of such changes? In Chapters Five and Six, time was important but in a different way. In these chapters we were interested in the extent of unity or oneness present in the relationships a person has. As our work progressed, then, the focus shifted to the problem of how to produce involvement over time in a person's life. The monograph began with a theory of what will produce the experience of involvement and ended with the question: What will produce an involved life?

The previous two chapters hopefully contributed to our understanding of how various forms of organizations and the mass media are overcoming the alienating effects of industrialization and urbanization and are helping people to experience their world as a unity.

In this concluding chapter we do not intend to restate points already made in previous chapters. However, there were three themes running throughout the work, and it is necessary now to pull together the information contained in the separate chapters on these three topics. The questions that continually shaped our analysis are: a) Are the perceptual categories of white and black, young and old, meaningful, i.e., are whites different from blacks in terms of the variables studied in this work, and are young people different from the old in terms of involvement? and b) What are the effects of mobility on involvement?

Finally, in this chapter we want to develop further the idea of artificial involvement discussed in the last chapter. It is hoped that this discussion will pave the way for future studies of involvement.

COLOR AND INVOLVEMENT

It must be remembered that our sample is entirely female and resided in a single section of Milwaukee. To what extent are there differences between the white and the black women living in Kilbourntown?

Color does not seem to contribute significantly to the tendency to think about dead people or to the tendency to think about people rarely seen, or to the number of blanks on the "think about" question, or to national involvement.

On the other hand there are differences between the color aggregates. Of relatively minor importance are the following: 1) Blacks have slightly less overlap between fantasy and household. 2) There is a slight tendency for blacks to seek more help on money and family problems (although this is not true at all age levels), but when they seek help the black women are less likely to go to their husbands. 3) The white women are a little less ignorant of their children's friends; 4) overall, blacks voted more often in the 1964 Presidential election. Although these differences are slight, several of them point to greater alienation within the black household, e.g., to less overlap of fantasy and household, less use of spouse as problem-solver, and less knowledge of children's lives. On the other hand the black women seem more involved outside the household, e.g., they more often seek help on problems and more of them voted.

Major differences between the color aggregates relate to family and religion. The whites' fantasy is much more restricted to the nuclear family, while black women have a fantasy life populated often by members of the extended family.

Regarding religion, there can be no doubt that religion plays a more significant role in the lives of black women. The facts are these: a) Blacks mentioned religious leaders on the "think about" question; thirteen of fourteen such references are by black people; b) Blacks more often express pride in their religious involvement (this is mainly true for those forty years of age and over); and c) Blacks more frequently attend church services (if the categories of "no attendance" and "rare attendance" are combined, then among those seventeen to thirty-nine years 9 percent more whites are infrequent attenders, among those forty to fifty-nine years 8 percent more whites are infrequent attenders, and among those sixty and above the percentage is 18 percent. The relevant data is contained in Table 5-6). Overall, the data suggest that although there is only a slight difference between whites and blacks in church attendance, there is a major difference in the degree to which religion permeates the daily lives of the respondents. For black people religion seems more personally meaningful. However, this seems to be true mainly for the middle-aged and older black women.

Overall, the data do suggest that black women may be less involved in household life. But it also suggests that the black women in our sample are more involved outside the household—in the extended family, in the nation, and in religion. At least in our sample, black women seems to lead richer lives in the sense that their horizons seem to embrace a more varied environment. But our work can only be suggestive.

But perhaps what needs to be emphasized most is that in our study color itself is not a very significant variable. At times there are no differences between blacks and whites, and when there are differences usually they are slight or not consistent for different ages. Of course our conclusions refer only to the types of variables studied in this work and to our limited sample.

AGE AND INVOLVEMENT

As Table 3-13 reveals, white women seventy-five years of age and older have a relatively low degree of involvement with their sensed environment. This is measured by the importance of dead people in their lives as well as by the absence of people thought about. As would be expected the elderly experience the least amount of overlap between fantasy and household.[1] Moreover, only 30 percent voted in 1964, and few seek help on either money or family problems. It must be remembered that there are only twenty cases of elderly white women in our sample. But there seems adequate basis for describing these women as alienated or disengaged.

Townsend and Tunstall summarized their work on national samples of people sixty-five and over and living in private households as follows; "We considered whether people disengage from society in advanced old age. We found that in all three countries [Britain, U.S., and Denmark] substantially more people in their 80's than in their late 60's are living alone and say they are often alone. But the trend towards isolation with age is not steep, and on none of our measures are more than two-fifths of those in their 80's 'isolated' or alone. ... Moreover, there is some evidence that when people become widowed or infirm they move to join their children."[2] The information derived from their study, however, seems rather superficial. e.g., whether a person lives alone or not, frequency of contact with others, self-perception as a lonely person. Such indicators reveal the minimum of alienation. If variables such as those used in our study were employed, these national samples would have appeared even more disengaged.

Of course our small sample of elderly white women in no way can be considered typical of elderly people. These women are slum-dwellers, not middle-class Americans. But at least for this sample the idea of disengagement seems more appropriate than intimacy-at-a-distance. It may be true, as argued by Rosenmayr and Kocheis, that elderly people prefer social arrangements that allow both involvement and independence.[3] But whether this is true or not, our data certainly do suggest that Cumming's theory of disengagement is valid. Elderly people do seem more alienated. Moreover, the simple fact that one source of alienation is involvement with dead people suggests that elderly people in all social classes are likely to feel more alienated than younger people.

We prefer the word "alienation" rather than "disengagement," The latter adequately expresses decline in involvement, but it fails to express the problems associated with a shift of involvement from the living to the dead. Alienation, on the other hand, is a richer concept. It can refer to the two somewhat distinct processes that seem to characterize our elderly women: 1) a decline of involvement, and 2) a shift of involvement from people in the sensed environment to non-sensed objects. Both processes contribute to the alienation of the elderly.

Regarding some variables it does not do justice to the data to talk about a process of aging, because both the very young and the old are similar. Consider, for example, the percent of people our respondents think about and with whom they discuss personal problems (Table 4-9). On this variable both those in their twenties and those seventy-five and over are low relative to the middle-aged. We can imagine, therefore, that elderly people will be especially prone to feeling alienated because they may experience a decline in the amount of personal communication they have with the people they think about. The amount of communication these elderly people carry on may be the same as that characteristic of young people. But the elderly may experience a greater sense of alienation because they had gone through the richer period of middle life.

As Townsend and Tunstall wrote—"Loneliness is related more to 'loss' than to enduring 'isolation'."[4] In part, the sense of alienation of the elderly can be blamed on the degree of involvement experienced in middle life.

The alienation of the elderly, therefore, must be seen as resulting from; 1) a withdrawal of involvement, 2) a shift of involvement to non-sensed objects,[5] and 3) the loss of the relatively rich life of the middle years. Recall, also, that expressed pride in health increased as age increased. This suggests a fourth reason for the social alienation of the elderly; 4) an increased involvement in the body. Of course, not all elderly people have this bodily involvement. We mention it as one of the bases for the social alienation of old people.

In evaluating the data in our study related to age, it must be kept in mind that we have not followed the same people through the various life stages, but only studied different people of varied ages.

MOBILITY AND INVOLVEMENT

The data scattered throughout the work *suggest* three different relations between mobility and involvement: 1) It was found that women who have lived in more cities or towns more often than the less mobile women indicated they are involved with their spouse; in short, some support was found for Bott's hypothesis that there is a positive relation between continuity of association and involvement; 2) On the other hand. the data on seeking help for financial and family problems *suggest* a settling-in, closing-out process; that is, there is a tendency for fewer long-term residents to seek help from others. It is possible that lengthy residence gives people confidence and security that allows them to solve their own problems; as people settle-in, they close out others; and 3) The data support the idea that newcomers are less often involved in the institutional life of an area. More specifically, newcomers less often attend church and fewer of them voted. It was suggested that if people are not stable, much of life seems indistinguishable from a novel, and action loses its urgency.

Quite tentatively we put forward the following model of mobile women; 1) highly involved with their spouses; 2) seek help mainly from family and friends with their problems,[6] which results in important but temporary (or intermittent) relations; infrequent involvement in community institutions. It follows that stable people would be less involved with their spouse, have fewer personally important relations and more socially important relations, i.e., relations that are continuous and which, therefore, are important for the preservation of the social system of which the relations are parts. Relative to mobile people, stable individuals would be more involved with themselves, i.e., not dependent on others for help; moreover, they would participate in more relationships that, however, would tend to be less personal than the relations of mobile people. In effect, we are suggesting that the individual transition from mobile to stable is similar to the historic transition from *Gemeinschaft* to *Gesellschaft*. If this is true, it means that the more mobile the population of a society, the more *Gemeinschaft*-like becomes the experience of its members. These ideas go well beyond our data. But we believe they are interesting and merit further consideration. We might ask, for instance, if the contempo-

		LOW	HIGH
	LOW	ALIENATED PERSON	ARTIFICIAL PERSON
POTENTIAL INVOLVEMENT			
	HIGH	ROBOTIC PERSON	INVOLVED PERSON

rary interest in community is due more to a reaction by stable people against impersonal relationships or to the desire of mobile people who live in a more personal world to want to build institutions that will allow them to continue their personal world after they settle down.[7] Or, is it true that mobile people will value individualism in the sense of being free to become involved whenever and with whomever they decide, while stable people will value individualism in the sense of self-determination, i.e., in the sense of not being dependent on others? The former would accept dependence, if it is freely chosen; the latter would reject all dependence.

ARTIFICIAL INVOLVEMENT

In the last chapter the idea of artificial involvement was introduced, it refers to involvement without adequate bases for the involvement. The self-image would be of an involved person, but there would be no adequate basis for this, and, we believe, the involvement would not affect major decisions since its artificiality would be experienced at some level of consciousness. Note that artificial involvement is not the same as the situation that arises when a person's subjective involvement is not consistent with his potential involvement because of a mistaken understanding about the degree of potential involvement. Artificial involvement is not based on a mistake. Artificial involvement could result, for instance, from propaganda. The recognition that the amount of potential involvement (i.e., closeness, similarity, power, and knowledge) and actual involvement do not always co-vary in anything like a perfect way led us to construct a typology contained in Diagram 7-1. Taking the involved type as the ideal, we see that there are three problem types: the alienated, the artificial, and the robotic.

The last type is new to our discussion but not to other analyses of contemporary culture. The prototype is the "hero" of Camus's novel *The Stranger,* but analyses of psychopathic personalities also reveal this syndrome of potential but not actual involvement. Below are comments made by a woman who supposedly had been helped by a psychiatrist:

"Well I don't have any desires now. I used to want Alice to be shown up in her true colors, to have people see how wrong she was. Now I just don't think about it. I just act. I get along."

"I still may think that what she's doing is wrong at times, but it doesn't matter much. That is, well, I would defend myself if she did anything wrong to me... but, well, I wouldn't *dwell* on its being wrong. I'm just not involved. It doesn't matter in the same way."

"It's funny, but if anyone ever looked at what I've said, they'd get the impression of a very strange and quiet person without real emotion, someone who didn't care about anything. That's not a good picture of me at all. It's true it takes a lot more effort to get angry now, and yet I explode all the time. The difference is that I used to get angry all the time and never exploded. Now, when I'm angry, I explode and yell, but somehow I'm not really ever worked up about it."[8]

It is difficult to conclude anything about this person simply from these quotations. But these statements are troublesome. They suggest a person who remains objectively related but who is subjectively detached.

Why the label "robotic"? The type of person we are referring to is like a machine that experiences bases of involvement, but bases that never coalesce to form a new fact—a sense of involvement. Robots will on occasion have knowledge of people, for instance, but this information will not produce a sense of involvement. Robotic people develop the potential for involvement, but never experience a sense of involvement.

A thorough analysis then of the contemporary world must acknowledge the existence of three problem-types: the alienated, the artificial, and the robotic. Each problem-type is a deviation from the original theory presented in Chapter One. There it was suggested that involvement varies with proximity, similarity, power, and knowldege. Now, we are acknowledging that without these bases, there can be involvement (artificial) and that these bases can exist without causing involvement (robotic). Future theoretical development will have to specify the conditions under which artificial involvement or roboticism will develop.

Notes

CHAPTER 1

1. Emile Durkheim, *The Division of Labor in Society* (New York: The Free Press, 1964), p. 14.

2. Quoted in: Elsworth Faris, "The Primary Group: Essence and Accident," *American Journal of Sociology* 28 (July 1932): 41.

3. Max Weber, *The Theory of Social and Economic Organization* (New York; The Free Press, 1966), p. 136.

4. Faris, "The Primary Group," p. 50.

5. Weber, *Social and Economic Organization,* p. 120.

6. Albert N. Cousins, "The Failure of Solidarity," in *The Family,* eds. Norman W. Bell and Ezra F. Vogel (Glencoe: The Free Press, 1960), p. 403.

7. From our perspective, Maslow's work is interesting because his concern about "peak-experience" underscores the fact that modern man is relatively cut off from his environment. On the other hand, Maslow's discussion of the "peak-experience" suffers from a failure to stress the neutral quality of involvement itself, and thus to distinguish the conditions under which oneness is creative from those under which it is destructive. Abraham Maslow, *Religions, Values, and Peak-Experiences* (Columbus: Ohio State University Press, 1964).

8. Robert Sommer and Humphrey Osmond, "The Schizophrenic No-Society," *Psychiatry* 25 (August 1962): 247.

9. Bruno Bettelheim, "Individual and Mass Behavior in Extreme Situations," in *Readings in Social Psychology,* eds. Elinore Maccoby, et. al. (New York: Holt, 1958), pp. 300-310.

10. For an explicit statement of the relative aspect of morale see: Aaron J. Spector, "Expectations, Fulfillment, and Morale," *Journal of Abnormal and Social Psychology* 52 (January 1956): 51-56. Unfortunately, alienation, the opposite of involvement, has sometimes been defined relatively; for example, Levin considered that the "felt discrepancy between what is and what might be is the hallmark of one's state of being-in-the-world," and that this feeling could be considered alienation. The term alienation has become linked with industrialization and often means not only the nature of the relation between a man and his products, but also the the frustrations associated with the life of a worker in an industrialized world. It would seem beneficial, however, to reserve the term alienation for the analysis of relationships, and morale for the discussion of frustrations. Murray Levin, *The Alienated Worker* (New York: Holt, Rinehart and Winston, 1962), p. 59. See also:

John P. Clark, "Measuring Alienation Within a Social System," *American Sociological Review* 24 (December 1959): 849-852.

11. For a general discussion of "integration" see: Werner S. Landecker, "Types of Integration and Their Measurement," *American Sociological Review* 61 (January 1951): 332-340.

12. Bernard Berelson and Gary A. Steiner, *Human Behavior* (New York: Harcourt, Brace and World, 1962), p. 106.

13. C. R. Carpenter, "Societies of Monkeys and Apes," in *Primate Social Behavior*, ed. Charles Southwick (Princeton: D. Van Nostrand, 1963), p. 6.

14. Other authors have pointed out that for some species distance from a certain point of common orientation is an indication of the amount of power an animal has within the group. Robert Ardrey, "The Drive for Territory," *Life* (26 August 1966): 40-58; Edward T. Hall, *The Hidden Dimension* (Garden City: Doubleday, 1966).

15. Durkheim, *Division of Labor;* Sigmund Freud, "On Narcissism: An Introduction," *Collected Papers,* vol. 4 (New York: Basic Books, 1959), p. 47; Ferdinand Toennies, *Community and Society* (New York: Harper Torchbook, 1963), p. 252. Frederick summarized the historical discussion of the meaning of community as follows; "first, there is the debate as to whether community in the first instance simply exists, or whether it is willed. Secondly, there is the debate over whether community, other values apart, is primarily a community of law or of love. Thirdly, there is the debate over whether community is organic or purposive." "Willed," "law," and "purposive" refer to systems based on power; the other terms are more ambiguous, but seem to imply the nonrational attraction that Toennies discussed and which occurs in groups connected via similarity or where the ethos is one of fundamental identity of the members of the group because of common blood. Carl Frederick, "The Concept of Community in the History of Political and Legal Philosophy," in *Community,* ed. Carl Frederick (New York: Liberal Arts Press, 1959), pp. 23-24.

16. Kurt Wolff, *The Sociology of Georg Simmel* (Glencoe: The Free Press, 1950), p. 307.

17. Toennies, *Community,* p.384.

18. Aristotle and, following him, Aquinas had a somewhat similar theory of relation; they clearly recognized the importance of knowledge, but merely pointed to similarity and power rather than clearly recognizing them. See: *The Great Books of the Western World* (Chicago: Encyclopedia Britannica, 1952) vol. 8, Aristotle, *Metaphysics,* 5: 15, and vol. 19, Thomas Aquinas, *The Summa Theologica,* 1: 13: 7. Hume, on the other hand, seems to have missed the significance of knowledge, but did realize the importance of contiguity, similarity, and less clearly perhaps, power. *Ibid.,* vol. 35, Hume, An Enquiry Concerning Human Understanding, p. 458.

19. Erving Goffman, *Behavior in Public Places* (New York: The Free Press, 1963), p. 124.

20. Joseph B. Tamney, "A Study of Involvement: Reactions to the Death of President Kennedy," *Sociologus* 19 (1969): 66-79.

21. Elaine Cumming, "Further Thoughts on the Theory of Disengagement,' *International Social Science Journal* 15 (1963): 377-378.

22. *Ibid.,* p. 380, footnote 3.

23. In the terms of Back and Gergen, old people have a smaller "effective life space." By this phrase these authors mean "the extent to which the person is willing to accept something as relevant to his conduct (including any facts about the world—past, present, and future)." Kurt W. Back and Kenneth J. Gergen, "Ageing and Self Orientation," in *Social Aspects of Ageing,* eds. Ida Harper Simpson and John C. McKinney (Durham: Duke University Press, 1966), p. 292.

24. Cumming, "Theory of Disengagement," p. 391, footnote 3.

25. *Ibid.,* p. 387.

26. *Ibid.,* p.381.

27. Leopold Rosenmayr and Eva Kockeis, "Propositions For a Sociological Theory of Ageing,"

International Social Science Journal 15 (1963): 418.

28. Cumming, "Theory of Disengagement," p. 382.

29. Norval D. Glenn and Michael Grimes, "Ageing, Voting, and Political Interest," *American Sociological review* 33 (August 1968). 565-571.

30. David O. Moberg, "Religiosity in Old Age," in *Middle Age and Ageing,* ed. Bernice C. Newgarten (Chicago: University of Chicago Press, 1968), p. 508.

CHAPTER 2

1. About 40 percent were two stories high, 8 percent were two and one-half stories, 21 percent had only one floor and 16 percent had one and one-half floors. A few buildings had three or four floors; there was inadequate information on about 13 percent of the buildings. Kilbourntown probably had much more variability in building size than a typical middle-class neighborhood. This variety contributed to the visual breaking up of the area.

Moreover, about 11 percent of the buildings had commercial enterprises; 77 percent were residential units. (There was inadequate information on about 12 percent of the buildings.) Again, this contributed to a sense of variety and a lack of unity.

2. This part of the city averages about 550 trees per quarter-mile; the city average is 1200; the desired average is 900. Data from Department of Parks and Streets, City of Milwaukee.

3. Data from Police Department and Office of the Clerk of Courts, City of Milwaukee.

4. Alex P. Dobish, "Young Hoodlums Rule by Fear in Area of Wells Street Schools," *Milwaukee Journal,* 11 October 1966.

5. Included in the study are female breadwinners; their main sources of income are as follows: job—86 (36 percent), social security—34 (14 percent), welfare—89 (37 percent), pension—2 (1 percent), other government programs—11 (5 percent), miscellaneous private sources—7 (3 percent), no response—9 (4 percent).

6. For a discussion of this see: Kenneth J. Gergen, "The Significance of Skin Color in Human Relations," *Daedalus* 96 (Spring 1967); 390-403.

7. As one would suspect for a mobile population, few, about 14 percent, owned the building in which they lived. (There was inadequate data on 12 percent of our sample. Our information on ownership is only approximate. The question was not asked in the interview. Our information comes from the city taxroll, which listed ownership as of December, 1966, i.e., about six months after the interviews were made. We compared the surname of respondent with the person taxed for the property. Our percentage is probably fairly accurate, however, because at the time of the interviews the buildings were "condemned" for renewal, and the owners were waiting to sell their property to the government.)

8. Eugene Litwak, "Geographical Mobility and Family Cohesion," *American Sociological Review* 25 (June 1960) 385-394; Elizabeth Bott, "Urban Families: Conjugal Roles and Social Networks," *Human Relations* 7 (1954); 372; Marvin B. Sussman and Lee G. Burchinal, "Kin Family Network: Unheralded Structure in Current Conceptualizations of Family Function," *Marriage and Family Living* 24 (August 1962): 231-240.

9. The percentage is based on the number of respondents who told us their income. The data on income cannot be considered precise information. Total family income is difficult for anyone to state precisely. On the other hand, the categories used are fairly broad. We assume that people were able to pick the right category even if they could not state their family's precise income. There is the additional problem, however, that people tend to overestimate their income, we could do nothing about that in our study.

CHAPTER 3

1. It is difficult to determine the reliability of open-ended questions. In this case, however, about

forty black women in our sample were interviewed, as part of another study, some two months after the first interview. They were asked—"Name the three people whom you think about most." About 40 percent of the individuals named were also named in our study. In the reinterview the "think about" question followed a long series of questions on the respondent's household. As could be expected, the main reason for the differences in the people named on the two occasions was that in the reinterview the respondents named more household members. In short, it appears that the "think about" question was influenced in the reinterview by its location in the questionnaire. We believe that the list of people named in our study is a more valid indicator of involvement because the question appeared in a more neutral context. In our study, the "think about" question followed questions on whether the respondent was born in a rural or urban area, her mobility and her memberships in voluntary associations. Admittedly, no context is completely neutral.

2. We have already noted the reliability problem with regard to open-ended questions. There is also the problem of interviewer differences in pursuing answers, especially for our study, which used indigenous personnel. Analysis of the frequency of "no response" by interviewer revealed some clearly abnormal frequencies. Since respondents were not randomly distributed among interviewers, these differences might be "real". But we cannot overlook the problem of interviewer differences; obviously the analysis of the distribution of involvement must be considered crude.

Another problem with open-ended questions concerns the ability to verbalize; "no responses" might reflect difficulties in communicating with the interviewer. We did relate "no responses" on the pride question with the years of schooling; there was no significant relation except for those with thirteen years of schooling or more, few of whom did not respond; however, there are only twenty-five such cases in our sample.

3. Jerome L. Singer, *Daydreaming* (New York: Random House, 1966), p. 57.

4. *Ibid.,* p. 59.

5. Eugene Litwak, "Geographical Mobility and Family Cohesion," *American Sociological Review* 25 (June 1960): 385-394; James S. Brown et. al., "Kentucky Mountain Migration and the Stem Family: An American Variation on a Theme by La Play," *Rural Sociology* 28 (March 1963): 48-69; Charles Tilly and C. Harold Brown, "On Uprooting, Kinship and the Auspices of Migration," *International Journal of Comparative Sociology* 8 (1967): 164.

A failure to answer the "proud" question does not mean the same thing as not answering the "think about" question. The latter can mean the absence of involvement in valued objects. A person may not be proud of anything because: 1) He is not involved in anything, 2) He does not value anything, or 3) Although he is involved, he is not involved in anything that is also valued. Clearly, involvement and pride are related but are independent. Therefore, we have not used the absence of pride as an indicator of the absence of involvement.

6. There are twenty-three respondents proud about a specific church; three of these are whites in their sixties. The remaining twenty responses are spread evenly among the various black age aggregates. In every respect, religion appears to be more central to the lives of black people.

7. Gary T. Marx, "Religion: Opiate or Inspiration of Civil Rights Militancy Among Negroes," *American Sociological Review* 32 (February 1967): 68.

8. But what is the effect on black people that the God of Christianity is almost always portrayed as white? Will the "black is beautiful" idea weaken or destroy the significance of Christianity for black people?

9 Lucien Levy-Bruhl, *The Soul of the Primitive* (New York: Frederick A. Praeger, 1966), p. 340.

10. Peter Townsend with the assistance of Sylvia Tunstall, "Isolation, Disolation and Loneliness," in *Old People in Three Industrial Societies,* ed. Ethel Shanas et. al. (London: Routledge and Kegan Paul, 1968), p. 276.

11. This was determined by taking those who said they have lived in only one city; this was double-checked by matching their reported age and their reported years lived in Milwaukee; since

we used five year intervals for the last two variables, a few cases might have been inappropriately considered life-time residents; if there was a discrepancy between age and years in Milwaukee, the cases were excluded.

12. Julio Cortazar, *Hopscotch* (New York: Pantheon, 1966), p. 96.

13. William Kornhauser, *The Politics of Mass Society* (London: Routledge & Kegan Paul, 1960), p. 75.

CHAPTER 4

1. The fact that middle-aged white women appear more deeply involved in their children could be an artifact of the wording of our question. The "think about" question limited respondents to only three people. If middle-aged black women were involved with many people including their children very deeply, because the question limited them to only three people, there would be times when these mothers would not mention their children despite their high involvement with them. As a matter of fact, however, middle-aged black women have a rather high percentage of blanks (18 percent) on the "think about" question; the percentage for whites is about the same. There seems no basis for believing, then, that middle-aged blacks are involved with more people than middle-aged whites.

The higher percentage of white children who are fantasy figures could be due not to the fact that white mothers are involved with more children, but to the fact that they have a lower total of fantasy figures. In fact, however, the middle-aged whites have a higher total that their black counterparts. (See Table 3-11).

2. Bert N. Adams, *Kinship in an Urban Setting* (Chicago: Markham, 1968), p. 169.

3. Charles Bowerman and Donald P. Irish, "Some Relationships of Stepchildren to their Parents," *Marriage and Family Living* 24 (May 1962): 113-128.

4. Robert O. Blood and Donald M. Wolfe, *Husbands and Wives* (Glencoe: The Free Press, 1960), pp. 159-161.

5. Elizabeth Bott, "Urban Families: Conjugal Roles and Social Networks," *Human Relations* 7 (1954): 372.

6. Eleanor Pavenstedt, "A Comparison of the Child-Rearing Environment of Upper, Lower and Very Low Lower Class Families," *American Journal of Orthopsychiatry* 35 (January 1965): 95.

7. Mirra Komarovsky, *Blue-Collar Marriage* (New York: Random House, Vintage Book Edition, 1967). p. 208.

8. Blood and Wolfe, *Husbands and Wives,* p. 149.

9. Nicholas Babchuk and Alan P. Bates, "The Primary Relations of Middle-Class Couples: A Study in Male Dominance," *American Sociological Review* 28 (June 1963): 379.

10. Komarovsky, *Blue-Collar Marriage,* pp. 112-113.

11. Sidney Jourard, "Self-Disclosure and Other Cathexis," *Journal of Abnormal and Social Psychology* 59 (1959): 431.

12. Blood and Wolfe, *Husbands and Wives,* p. 186.

13. Marvin B. Sussman, "Relationships of Adult Children with Their Parents in the United States," in *Social Structure and the Family: Generational Relations,* eds. Ethel Shanas and Gordon F. Streib (Englewood Cliffs: Prentice-Hall, 1965), p. 77.

14. Herbert Gans, *The Urban Villagers* (New York: The Free Press, 1962), p. 51.

15. Komarovsky, *Blue-Collar Marriage,* p. 338.

16. If the "think about" question is at all meaningful, there should be significant overlap between the people in our respondents' fantasy life and the people they seek advice from. For blacks, 34 percent of the people they seek help from are thought about; if we eliminate the nonpersonal sources of help (who would be more peripheral to our respondents' lives, i.e. who although sources of advice would probably exercise this power less frequently) the figure is 48 percent. For whites,

45 percent of their advisors are thought about, and if we eliminate the nonpersonal sources it is 58 percent. Clearly, this does suggest that the "think about" question is meaningful. It is, also, evident that there is more unity in the white world; more of their advisors are part of their fantasy world.

17. Our approach is similar to that of Fromm-Reichman who views loneliness as a lack of interpersonal intimacy. She also notes that loneliness is "one of the least satisfactorily conceptualized psychological phenomena, not even mentioned in most psychiatric textbooks." Frieda Fromm-Reichman, "Loneliness," *Psychiatry* 22 (February 1959): 1-16.

18. Eleanore Luckey, "Number of Years Married as Related to Personality Perception and Marital Satisfaction," *Journal of Marriage and the Family* 28 (February 1966): 44-48; Jourard, "Self-Disclosure."

19. Among the blacks there are ten handicapped children, i.e., children whose illnesses incapacitated them. For such children, ignorance is low; only one handicapped child's mother does not know the friend's name.

20. Reuben Hill, "Decision-Making and the Family Life Cycle," in *Social Structure,* eds. Shanas and Strieb, pp. 116-117.

21. This occurs earlier for blacks. The explanation might be as follows: a) for whites, nonhousehold children jump in importance when the spouse and siblings are dead; b) for blacks, children might become important when parents and aunts and uncles are dead; and since older members of the extended family die before spouses and siblings, the jump in importance of children occurs earlier for blacks.

CHAPTER 5

1. Harold L. Wilensky, "A Second Look at the Traditional View of Urbanism," in *Perspectives on the American Community: A Book of Readings,* ed. Roland C. Warren (Chicago: Rand McNally, 1966), p. 141.

2. Hans Paul Bahrdt, "Public Activity and Private Activity as Basic Forms of City Association," in *American Community,* ed. Warren, p. 83.

3. Wilensky, "A Second Look," p. 138.

4. Roland L. Warren, *The Community in America* (Chicago: Rand McNally, 1963), p. 240.

5. William F. Whyte, *Street Corner Society* (Chicago: University of Chicago Press, 1965), p. 255.

6. On this point the concept of advice-structure differs from Warren's idea of the "mutual support function". Bartenders can fulfill this function, but they would not be considered part of an advice-structure. The bartender-customer relation would be considered, by us, as part of the informal organization of Kilbourntown.

7. Warren, *The Community,* p. 196.

8. The figure of 9 percent assumes that a pair of respondents do not share more than one name on the "think about" question. But this did happen, so that the actual percentage of people sharing one or more names on the "think about" question is less than 9 percent.

9. In a few cases, the respondent mentioned not a name but a role, like "my social worker." Even if these roles all referred to the same person it would not affect the validity of our general conclusions.

10. Marvin Sussman and R. Clyde White, *Hough, Cleveland, Ohio: A Study of Social Life and Change* (Cleveland: The Press of Western Reserve University, 1959), pp. 91-2; quoted in Warren, *The Community,* p. 197.

11. Donald R. Matthews and James W. Prothro, *Negroes and the New Southern Politics* (New York: Harcourt, Brace and World, 1966), p. 180.

12. Warren, *The Community,* p. 172.

13. Suttles studied an ethnically mixed neighborhood in Chicago, and reported: "In all there are

ten separate places of worship in the area. None of them brings together different ethnic groups." Gerald D. Suttles, *The Social Order of the Slum* (Chicago: University of Chicago Press, 1968), p. 42.

14. Warren, *The Community,* p. 192.

15. Alphonso Pinkney, *Black Americans* (Englewood Cliffs: Prentice-Hall, 1969), pp. 112-113.

16. Warren, *The Community,* p. 194.

17. Religious voluntary associations that drew members from more than one church, however, were included in the analysis.

18. Nicholas Babchuk and Alan Booth, "Voluntary Association Membership: A Longitudinal Analysis," *American Sociological Review* 34 (February 1969): 31-45.

19. An important omission in our field work is the absence of information on the contribution of neighborhood bars to life in Kilbourntown. We know there are plenty of them, and we know from observation that they are frequented both day and night. These bars may not be too important, however, to female homemakers. But the important question is whether bar-life really changes anything. All forms of what Simmel called sociability produce temporary occasions of involvement with others. But does sociability in K-3 produce any lasting sense of a "common order" that could give a continuous sense of involvement? People who drink together can still remain "familiar strangers." In fact the impersonality of sociable events noted by Simmel contributes to experiencing others as "familial strangers." Do the bars in neighborhoods like Kilbourntown produce any lasting sense of involvement with others? Georg Simmel, "The Sociology of Sociability," in *Theories of Society,* eds. Talcott Parsons et.al. (Glencoe: The Free Press, 1961), pp. 157-163.

20. For further discussion of this see: Joseph B. Tamney, "The Prediction of Religious Change," *Sociological Analysis* 26 (Summer 1965): 72-81.

21. Michael Argyle, "Religious Observance," in *International Encyclopedia of the Social Sciences,* ed. David Sills (New York: Macmillan and The Free Press, 1968), vol. 13, pp. 421-428.

22. Dennison Nash and Peter Berger, "The Child, The Family and The 'Religious Revival' in Suburbia," *Journal for the Scientific Study of Religion* 2 (October 1962): 85-93.

23. Terrence Lee, "Urban Neighborhood as a Socio-Spatial Scheme," *Human Relations* 21 (1968): 259. Similarly, Nohara found that length of residence is related to neighborliness (as measured by number of best friends in the neighborhood, number of neighborhood homes visited, frequency of such visits, and number of neighbors' names known).

Specifically, he found that people living in the same dwelling unit three years or more are more often high on neighborliness than those who have lived in the same dwelling unit less than three years. Shigeo Nohara, "Social Context and Neighborliness: The Negro in St. Louis," in *The New Urbanization,* ed. Scott Greer et. al. (New York: St. Martins Press, 1968), pp. 179-188. See, also: Joel Smith et. al., "Local Intimacy in a Middle-Sized City," *American Journal of Sociology* 60 (November 1954): 276-284.

Recently, Litwak and Szelenyi have suggested that "short tenure can be partially compensated for by rapid means of indoctrination." They argue that "where the group norms state newcomers are to be welcomed and newcomers have norms that long-term residents are friends, speedy indoctrination is encouraged...." The authors seem to assume that if there are norms stating that a certain behavior is desirable, then that behavior will occur. But this is not always true. For instance, perhaps it takes people years to break old ties, and so be willing to become involved in a new neighborhood. Or, perhaps it takes years to collect enough information about others to consider them close friends. But the article by Litwak and Szelenyi points to a key issue: the extent to which the effects of mobility on involvement are controllable by social policy. Eugene Litwak and Ivan Szelenyi, "Primary Group Structures and Their Functions: Kin, Neighbors, and Friends," *American Sociological Review* 34 (August 1969): 467.

24. Jitodai in an analysis of over 3,000 white residents of Detroit found no relation between migratory status and frequency of church attendance after controlling for several key variables. However, in a subsample of Southern-born, white, non-Catholic females (this was the subsample closest to ours), there was a tendency for those who had lived less than twenty-five years in Detroit to attend church less frequently than those who had lived twenty-five years or more in Detroit; but some of the cells in this subanalysis are quite small. Jitodai's work, the results of which are not consistent with ours, implies that it is impossible yet to be certain about the effects of mobility on organizational participation. Ted T. Jitodai, "Migrant Status and Church Attendance," *Social Forces* 47 (December 1960): 241-248.

25. Our interest in voluntary associations has been from the perspective of whether or not they are significant sources of neighborhood structure. There is, of course, some research that suggests that not belonging to voluntary associations is associated with a general sense of powerlessness, which some authors call alienation. It should be noted, however, that these authors differ from us in their meaning of "alienation." Arthur C. Neal and Melvin Seeman, "Organizations and Powerlessness," *American Sociological Review* 29 (April 1964): 216-226; Joel I. Nelson, "Participation and Integration: The Case of the Small Businessman," *American Sociological Review* 33 (June 1968): 427-438.

26. James S. Coleman, "Community Disorganization," in *Contemporary Social Problems,* eds. Robert K. Merton and Robert A. Nisbet, 2nd ed. (New York: Harcourt, Brace and World, 1966), p. 709.

27. Christopher Alexander, "The City as a Mechanism for Sustaining Human Contact," in *Environment for Man,* ed. William R. Ewald. Jr. (Bloomington: Indiana University Press, 1969), p. 65.

28. The Open Group, "Social Reform in the Centrifugal Society," *New Society* 363 (11 September 1969): 389.

CHAPTER 6

1. In this chapter we have equated nation and state. This is not always legitimate. The assumption would probably not be valid for many South American countries, for instance, but we believe it is reasonable for the United States at this point in time.

2. H.H. Gerth and C. Wright Mills, *From Max Weber: Essays in Sociology* (New York: Oxford University Press, Galaxy Book, 1958), pp. 171-179.
Louis Wirth similarly linked nationalism with the struggle for status. Louis Wirth, "Types of Nationalism," *American Journal of Sociology* 41 (May 1936): 723-737.

3. Boyd C. Shafer, "Toward a Definition of Nationalism," in *Nationalism and International Progress.* ed. Urban G. Whitaker (San Francisco: Chandler, 1961). pp. 4-5.

4. Samuel A. Stouffer, *Communism, Conformity and Civil Liberties* (Gloucester, Massachusetts: Peter Smith, 1963), p. 130.

5. C. Vann Woodward, *The Burden of Southern History* (Baton Rouge: Louisiana State University Press, 1960), p. 15.

6. *Ibid.,* pp.23-24.

7. Karl W. Deutsch, *Nationalism and Social Communication,* 2nd ed. (Cambridge: M.I.T. Press, 1960), p. 97.

8. *Ibid.,* pp. 173-174.

9. Florian Znaniecki, *Modern Nationalities* (Urbana: University of Illinois Press, 1952), p. 22.

10. There also was a fictitious name, "Allen Garmon," on the questionnaire. Only twenty-eight people reported watching him, and for some of these a positive answer could be the result of an honest mistake. The other names were Red Skelton, Jack Benny, and Dean Martin.

11. For further discussion of some of the points raised in this paragraph see the following articles

in the *International Encyclopedia of the Social Sciences,* ed. David Sills (New York: Macmillan and The Free Press, 1968): Donald E. Stokes, "Voting," vol. 16, pp. 387-395; Herbert McClosky, "Political Participation," vol. 12, pp. 252-265.

12. Norval D. Glenn and Michael Grimes, "Ageing, Voting, and Political Interest," *American Sociological Review* 33 (August 1968): 563-575.

13. *Ibid.,* p. 575.

14. Angus Campbell et. al., *The American Voter* (New York: John Wiley, 1960), p. 139.

15. Donald R. Matthews and James W. Prothro. *Negroes and the New Southern Politics* (New York: Harcourt, Brace and World, 1966), p. 253.

16. See, for instance: Philip K. Hastings, "The Voter and the Non-Voter," *American Journal of Sociology* 62 (November 1965): 302-307; William Erbe, "Social Involvement and Political Activity: A replication and Elaboration," *American Sociological Review* 19 (April 1964): 198-215. This relation was also found to hold for a sample of black people in urban South Carolina: John B. McConaughy and John H. Gauntlett, "The Influence of the S Factor upon the Voting Behaviour of South Carolina Urban Negroes," *The Western Political Quarterly* 16 (December 1963): 973-984.

17. McClosky, "Political Participation," p. 257.

18. Melvin Seeman, "On the Personal Consequences of Alienation in Work," *American Sociological Review* 32 (April 1967): 273-286.

19. Erbe, "Social Involvement"; Joel I. Nelson, "Participation and Integration: The Case of the Small Businessman," *American Sociological Review* 33 (June 1968): p. 431, footnote 9.

20. Similarly Sharp found in a random sample of Detroit residents that the percentage voting increased continuously as the years lived in Detroit increased. Harry Sharp, "Migration and Voting Behavior in a Metropolitan Community," *Public Opinion Quarterly* 9 (Summer 1955): 204-209.

CHAPTER 7

1. Also among those 60-74 (there were insufficient cases of people over 74) there is a decline in the percent of married women who thinks about their spouse. In short, spousal involvement seems to decline among the old respondents. And, of course, maternal ignorance of the child's friend decreases at an early age (30 for blacks, 40 for whites).

2. Peter Townsend with the assistance of Sylvia Tunstall, "Isolation, Disolation and Loneliness," in *Old People in Three Industrial Societies,* eds. Ethel Shanas et. al. (London: Routledge and Kegan Paul, 1968), p. 286.

3. Leopold Rosenmayr and Eva Kockeis, "Propositions For a Sociological Theory of Ageing," *International Social Science Journal* 15 (1963): 410-426.

4. Townsend and Tunstall, "Isolation," p. 285.

5. The only form of involvement that significantly increases with age besides involvement with the dead is church attendance. This suggests the increasing importance of spiritual involvement which is a form of involvement with nonsensed objects.

6. What we mean is that more of the mobile women than of the stable women will do this; a majority of both types might never seek help.

7. This, in turn, leads to the larger question—does change come from those who are forced to endure inhuman lives or from those who experience a new life and are seeking to make it endure?

8. Herbert Fingarette, "The Ego and Mystic Selflessness," in *Anxiety and Identity,* eds. Maurice Stein and Arthur Vidich (Glencoe: The Free Press, 1960), p. 554.

Bibliography

Adams, Bert N. *Kinship in an Urban Setting.* Chicago: Markham, 1968.

Alexander, Christopher. "The City as a Mechanism for Sustaining Human Contact." In *Environment for Man,* edited by Willian R. Ewald, Jr., pp. 60-102. Bloomington: Indiana University Press, 1969.

Ardrey, Robert. "The Drive for Territory." *Life* (26 August 1966): 40-58.

Argyle, Michael. "Religious Observance." In *International Encyclopedia of the Social Sciences,* edited by David Sills, pp. 421-428, vol. 13. New York: Macmillan & The Free Press, 1968.

Babchuk, Nicholas and Bates, Alan P. "The Primary Relations of Middle-class Couples: A Study in Male Dominance.' *American Sociological Review* 28 (June 1963): 377-384.

Babchuk, Nicholas and Booth, Alan. "Voluntary Association Membership: A Longitudinal Analysis." *American Sociological Review* 34 (February 1969): 31-45.

Back, Kurt W. and Gergen, Kenneth J. "Ageing and Self Orientation." In section IV of *Social Aspects of Aging,* edited by Ida Harper Simpson and John C. McKinney. Durham: Duke University Press, 1966.

Bahrdt, Hans Paul, "Public Activity and Private Activity as Basic Forms of City Association." In *Perspective on the American Community: A Book of Readings,* edited by Ronald L. Warren, pp. 78-85. Chicago: Rand McNally, 1966.

Berelson, Bernard and Steiner, Gary A. *Human Behavior.* New York: Harcourt, Brace and World, 1962.

Bettleheim, Bruno. "Individual and Mass Behavior in Extreme Situations." In *Readings in Social Psychology,* edited by Elinore Maccoby, et al., pp. 300-310. 3rd ed. New York: Holt, 1958.

Blood, Robert O. and Wolfe, Donald M. *Husbands and Wives.* Glencoe: The Free Press, 1960.

Bott, Elizabeth, "Urban Families: Conjugal Roles and Social Networks." *Human Relations* 7 (1954): 345-384.

Bowerman, Charles and Irish, Donald P. "Some Relationships of Stepchildren to their Parents." *Marriage and Family Living* 24 (May 1962): 113-128.

Brown, James S., et al. "Kentucky Mountain Migration and the Stem Family: An American Variation on a Theme by La Play." *Rural Sociology* 28 (March 1963): 48-69.

Campbell, Angus. "The Passive Citizen." *Acta Sociologica* 6 (1962): 9-21.

Campbell, Angus, et al. *The American Voter.* New York: John Wiley, 1960.

Campbell, Angus. *Elections and Political Order.* New York: John Wiley, 1966.

Campbell, Donald T. "Common Fate, Similarity, and Other Indices of the Status of Aggregates of Persons as Social Entities." *Behavioral Science* 3 (June 1958): 14-25.

Carpenter, C.R. "Societies of Monkeys and Apes." In *Primate Social Behavior,* edited by Charles Southwick. Princeton: D. Van Nostrand, 1963.

Clark, John P. "Measuring Alienation Within a Social System." *American Sociological Review* 24 (December 1959): 849-852.

Coleman, James S. "Community Disorganization." In *Contemporary Social Problems,* edited by Robert K. Merton and Robert A. Nisbet, pp. 670-722. 2nd ed., New York: Harcourt, Brace & World, 1966.

Cortazar, Julio. *Hopscotch.* New York: Pantheon, 1966.

Cousins, Albert N. "The Failure of Solidarity." In *The Family,* edited by Norman W. Bell and Ezra F. Vogel, pp. 403-416. Glencoe: The Free Press 1960.

Cumming, Elaine. "Further Thoughts On The Theory of Disengagement." *International Social Science Journal* 15 (1963): 377-393.

Deutsch, Karl W. *Nationalism and Social Communication.* 2nd ed. Cambridge: M.I.T. Press, 1966.

Dobish, Alex P. "Young Hoodlums Rule by Fear in Area of Wells Street Schools." *Milwaukee Journal,* 11 October 1966.

Durkheim, Emile. *The Division of Labor in Society.* New York: The Free Press. 1964.

Erbe, William. "Social Involvement and Political Activity: A Replication and Elaboration." *American Sociological Review* 19 (April 1964): 198-215.

Faris, Elsworth. "The Primary Group: Essence and Accident." *American Journal of Sociology* 28 (July 1932): 41-50.

Fingarette, Herbert "The Ego and Mystic Selflessness." In *Anxiety and Identity,* edited by Maurice Stein and Arthur Vidich, pp. 552-585. Glencoe: The Free Press.

Frederick, Carl. "The Concept of Community in the History of Political and Legal Philosophy." In *Community,* edited by Carl Frederick. New York: Liberal Arts Press, 1959.

Freud, Sigmund. "On Narcissism: An Introduction." *Collected Papers.* vol. 4. New York: Basic Books, 1959.

Fromm-Reichman, Frieda. "Loneliness." *Psychiatry* 22 (February 1959): 1-16.

Gans, Herbert. *The Urban Villagers.* New York: The Free Press, 1962.

Gergen, Kenneth J. "The Significance of Skin Color in Human Relations." *Daedulus* 96 (Spring 1967): 390-403.

Gerth, H. H. and Mills, C. Wright. *From Max Weber: Essays in Sociology.* New York: Oxford University Press, Galaxy Book, 1958.

Glenn, Norval D. and Grimes, Michael. "Ageing, Voting, and Political Interest." *American Sociological Review* 33 (August 1968): 563-575.

Goffman, Erving. *Behavior in Public Places.* New York: The Free Press, 1963.

Hall, Edward T. *The Hidden Dimension.* Garden City: Doubleday, 1966.

Hastings, Philip K. "The Voter and the Non-Voter." *American Journal of Sociology* 62 (November 1965): 302-307.

Hatch, Robert. "Films." *The Nation* (September 22, 1969): 274-275.

Hill, Reuben, "Decision-Making and the Family Life Cycle." In *Social Structure and the Family: Generational Relations,* edited by Ethel Shanas and Gordon F. Streib, pp. 113-139. Englewood Cliffs: Prentice-Hall, 1965.

Hutchins, Robert Maynard, ed. *Critique of Pure Reason in Kant,* vol 42. *Aristotle,* vol.8. *Thomas Aquinas,* vol.19. *David Hume,* vol. 35. *Plato,* vol.7. The Great Books. Chicago: Encyclopedia Britannica, 1952.

Jitodai, Ted T. "Migrant Status and Church Attendance." *Social Forces* 47 (December 1960): 241-248.

Jourard, Sidney, *The Transparent Self.* Princeton: D. Van Nostrand, 1964.

Jourard, Sidney, and Lasakow, Paul. "Some Factors in Self-Disclosure." *Journal of Abnormal and Social Psychology* 56 (1958): 91-98.

Komarovsky, Mirra. *Blue-Collar Marriage.* New York: Random House, 1964. (Some references are to Vintage Book Edition, 1967.)

Kornhauser, William. *The Politics of Mass Society.* London: Routledge & Kegan Paul, 1960.

Landecker, Werner S. "Types of Integration and Their Measurement." *American Sociological Review* 61 (January 1951): 332-340.

Lee, Terrence. "Urban Neighborhood as a Socio-Spatial Scheme." *Human Relations* 21 (1968): 241-267.

Levin, Murray. *The Alienated Worker.* New York: Holt, Rinehart and Winston, 1962.

Levy-Bruhl, Lucien. *The Soul of the Primitive.* New York: Frederick A. Praeger, 1966.

Litwak, Eugene. "Geographical Mobility and Family Cohesion." *American Sociological Review* 25 (June 1960): 385-394.

Litwak, Eugene, and Szelenyi, Ivan. "Primary Group Structures and Their Functions: Kin, Neighbors, and Friends." *American Sociological Review* 34 (August 1969): 465-481.

Luckey, Eleanore. "Number of Years Married as Related to Personality Perception and Marital Satisfaction." *Journal of Marriage and the Family* 28 (February 1966): 44-48.

Maslow, Abraham. *Religions, Values, and Peak-Experiences.* Columbus: Ohio State University Press, 1964.

Marx, Gary T. "Religion: Opiate or Inspiration of Civil Rights Militancy Among Negroes." *American Sociological Review* 32 (1967): 64-72.

McConaughy, John B. and Gauntlett, John H. "The Influence of the S Factor upon the Voting Behaviour of South Carolina Urban Negroes." *The Western Political Quarterly* 16 (December 1963): 973-984.

McClosky, Herbert. "Political Participation." In *International Encyclopedia of the Social Sciences,* edited by David Sill, pp. 252-265. vol. 12. New York: Macmillan and The Free Press, 1968.

Nash, Dennison, and Berger, Peter. "The Child, The Family and The 'Religious Revival' in Suburbia." Journal for the Scientific Study of Religion 2 (October 1962): 85-93.

Moberg, David O. "Religiosity in Old Age." In *Middle Age and Ageing,* edited by Bernice C. Neugarter, pp. 497-508. Chicago: University of Chicago Press, 1968.

Neal, Arthur C., and Seeman, Melvin. "Organizations and Powerlessness." *American Sociological Review* 29 (April 1964): 216-226.

Nelson, Joel I. "Participation and Integration: The Case of the Small Businessman," *American Sociological Review* 33 (June 1968): 427-438.

Nohara, Shigeo. "Social Context and Neighborliness: The Negro in St. Louis." In *The New Urbanization,* edited by Scott Greer et al., pp. 179-188. New York: St. Martins Press, 1968.

Orum, Anthony. "A Reappraisal of Social and Political Participation." *American Journal of Sociology* 72 (March 1967): 32-46.

Pavenstedt, Eleanor. "A Comparison of the Child-Rearing Environment of Upper, Lower and Very Low Lower Class Families." *American Journal Of Orthopsychiatry* 35 (January 1965): 89-98.

Pinkney, Alphonso. *Black Americans.* Englewood Cliffs: Prentice-Hall, 1969.

Pinter, Frank A. "Cross Pressure." In *International Encyclopedia of the Social Sciences,* edited by David Sill, pp. 519-522. vol. 3. New York: Macmillan and The Free Press, 1968.

Rosenberg, Morris. "Some Determinants of Political Apathy" *Public Opinion Quarterly* 18 (1954-55): 349-366.

Rosenmayr, Leopold, and Kockeis, Eva. "Propositions For a Sociological Theory of Ageing." *International Social Science Journal* 15 (1963): 410-426.

Seeman, Melvin. "On the Personal Consequences of Alienation in Work." *American Sociological Review* 32 (April 1967): 273-286.

Shafer, Boyd C. "Toward a Definition of Nationalism." In *Nationalism and International Progress,* edited by Urban G. Whitaker. San Francisco: Chandler, 1961.

Sharp, Harry. "Migration and Voting Behavior in a Metropolitan Community." *Public Opinion Quarterly* 9 (Summer 1955): 204-209.

Shils, Edward. "Color, the Universal Intellectual Community, and the Afro-Asian Intellectual." *Daedalus* 96 (Spring 1967): 279-295.

Simmel, Georg. "The Sociology of Sociability." In *Theories of Society,* edited by Talcott Parsons, et al. pp. 157-163. vol. 2. Glencoe: The Free Press, 1961.

Singer, Jerome L. *Daydreaming.* New York: Random House, 1966.

Smith, Joel, et al. "Local Intimacy in a Middle-sized City." *American Journal of Sociology* 60 (November 1954): 276-284.

Sommer, Robert, and Osmond, Humphrey. "The Schizophrenic No-Society." *Psychiatry* 25 (August 1962): 244-255.

Spector, Aaron J. "Expectations, Fulfillment, and Morale." *Journal of Abnormal and Social Psychology* 52 (January 1956): 51-56.

Stokes, Donald E. "Voting." In *International Encyclopedia of the Social Science,* edited by David Sill, pp. 387-395. vol. 16. New York: Macmillan and The Free Press, 1968.

Stouffer, Samuel A. *Communism, Conformity and Civil Liberties.* Gloucester, Massachusetts: Peter Smith, 1963.

Strauss, Anselm, *The Social Psychology of George Herbert Mead.* Chicago: University of Chicago Press, 1956.

Sussman, Marvin B., and Burchinal, Lee G. "Kin Family Network: Unheralded Structure in Current Conceptualizations of Family Function." *Marriage and Family Living* 24 (August 1962): 231-240.

Sussman, Marvin, and White, R. Clyde. *Hough, Cleveland, Ohio: A Study of Social Life and Change.* Cleveland: The Press of Western Reserve University, 1959.

Tamney, Joseph B. "The Prediction of Religion Change." *Sociological Analysis* 26 (Summer 1965): 72-81.

———. "A Study of Involvement: Reactions to the Death of President Kennedy." *Sociologus* 19 (1969): 66-79.

Tilly, Charles, and Brown, C. Harold. "On Uprooting, Kinship and the Auspices of Migration." *International Journal of Comparative Sociology* 8 (1967): 139-164.

The Open Group. "Social Reform in the Centrifugal Society." *New Society* 363 (11 September 1969): 387-395.

Toennies, Ferdinand. *Community and Society.* New York: Harper Torchbook, 1963.

Townsend, Peter with the assistance of Sylvia Tunstall. "Isolation, Disolation and Loneliness." In *Old People in Three Industrial Societies,* edited by Ethel Shanas. et al., pp. 258-287. London: Routledge and Kegan Paul, 1968.

Warren, Roland L. *The Community in America.* Chicago: Rand McNally, 1963.

Weber, Max. *The Theory of Social and Economic Organization.* New York: The Free Press, 1966.

Whyte, William F. *Street Corner Society.* Chicago: University of Chicago Press, 1965.

Wilensky, Harold L. "A Second Look at the Traditional View of Urbanism." In *Perspectives on the American Community: A Book of Readings,* edited by Roland C. Warren, pp. 135-147. Chicago: Rand McNally, 1966.

Wirth, Louis. "Types of Nationalism." *American Journal of Sociology* 41 (May 1936): 723-737.

Wolff, Kurt. *The Sociology of Georg Simmel.* Glencoe: The Free Press, 1950.

Woodward, C. Vann. *The Burden of Southern History.* Baton Rouge: Louisiana State University Press, 1960.

Znaniecki, Florian. *Modern Nationalities.* Urbana, University of Illinois Press, 1952.

INDEX